NEW DIRECTIONS 38

New Directions in Prose and Poetry 38

Edited by J. Laughlin

with Peter Glassgold and Frederick R. Martin

A New Directions Book

Library of Congress Catalog Card Number: 37–1751 (Serial)

ACKNOWLEDGMENTS
Lawrence Ferlinghetti's "Second Populist Manifesto: Adieu à Charlot" was first published in *City Lights Journal* (Number 4, Spring 1978), Copyright © 1978 by Lawrence Ferlinghetti.

William Heinesen's "The Flies" (*"Fluerne"*) originates from the volume *Kur mod onde Ander* ("Cure Against Evil Spirits"), © William Heinesen, published by Gyldendal, Copenhagen.

"The Snowflakes of Giordan Bruno," by Dick Higgins, Copyright © 1977 by Dick Higgins.

"Blues for a Black Cat," by Boris Vian, was first published in French by Editions le Terrain Vague, Paris.

Manufactured in the United States of America
First published clothbound (ISBN: 0–8112–0710–2) and New Directions Paperbook 471 (ISBN: 0–8112–0711–0) in 1979

New Directions Books are published for James Laughlin
by New Directions Publishing Corporation,
80 Eighth Avenue, New York 10011

CONTENTS

SECOND POPULIST MANIFESTO: ADIEU À CHARLOT

LAWRENCE FERLINGHETTI

Sons of Whitman sons of Poe
sons of Lorca & Rimbaud
or their dark daughters
poets of another breath
poets of another vision
Who among you still speaks of revolution
Who among you still unscrews
the locks from the doors
in this revisionist decade?
'You are President of your own body, America'
Thus spoke Kush in Tepotzlan
youngblood wildhaired angel poet
one of a spawn of wild poets
in the image of Allen Ginsberg
wandering the wilds of America
'You Rimbauds of another breath'
sang Kush
and wandered off with his own particular paranoias
maddened like most poets
for one mad reason or another

in the unmade bed of the world
Sons of Whitman
in your 'public solitude'
bound by blood-duende
'President of your own body America'
Take it back from those who have maddened you
back from those who stole it
and steal it daily
The subjective must take back the world
from the objective gorillas & guerrillas of the world
We must rejoin somehow
the animals in the fields
in their steady-state meditation
'Your life is in your own hands still
Make it flower make it sing'
(so sang mad Kush in Tepotzlan)
'a constitutional congress of the body'
still to be convened to seize control
of the State
the subjective state
from those who have subverted it
The arab telephone of the avant-garde
has broken down
And I speak to you now
from another country
Do not turn away
in your public solitudes
you poets of other visions
of the separate lonesome visions
untamed uncornered visions
fierce recalcitrant visions
you Whitmans of another breath
which is not the too-cool breath of modern poetry
which is not the halitosis of industrial civilization
Listen now Listen again
to the song in the blood the dark duende a dark singing
between the tickings of civilization
between the lines of its headlines
in the silences between cars

driven like weapons
In two hundred years of freedom
we have invented
the permanent alienation of the subjective
almost every truly creative being
alienated & expatriated
in his own country
in Middle America or San Francisco
the death of the dream in your birth
o meltingpot America
I speak to you
from another country
another kind of blood-letting land
from Tepotzlan the poets' lan'
Land of the Lord of the Dawn
Quetzalcoatl
Land of the Plumed Serpent
I signal to you
as Artaud signalled
through the flames
I signal to you
over the heads of the land
the hard heads that stand like menhirs
above the land in every country
the short-haired hyenas
who still rule everything
I signal to you from Poets' Land
you poets of the alienated breath
to take back your land again
and the deep sea of the subjective
Have you heard the sound of the ocean lately
the sound by which daily
the stars still are driven
the sound by which nightly
the stars retake their sky
The sea thunders still to remind you
of the thunder in the blood
to remind you of your selves
Think now of your self

as of a distant ship
Think now of your beloved
of the eyes of your beloved
whoever is most beloved
he who held you hard in the dark
or she who washed her hair by the waterfall
whoever makes the heart pound
the blood pound
Listen says the river
Listen says the sea Within you
you with your private visions
of another reality a separate reality
Listen and study the charts of time
Read the sanskrit of ants in the sand
You Whitmans of another breath
there is no one else to tell
how the alienated generations
have lived out their expatriate visions
here and everywhere
The old generations have lived them out
Lived out the bohemian myth in Greenwich Villages
Lived out the Hemingway myth
in *The Sun Also Rises*
at the Dôme in Paris
or with the bulls at Pamplona
Lived out the Henry Miller myth
in the *Tropics* of Paris
and the great Greek dream
of *The Colossus of Maroussi*
and the tropic dream of Gauguin
Lived out the D. H. Lawrence myth
in *The Plumed Serpent*
in Mexico Lake Chapalla
And the Malcolm Lowry myth
Under the Volcano at Cuernavaca
And then the saga of *On the Road*
and the Bob Dylan myth Blowing in the Wind
How many roads must a man walk down
How many Neal Cassadys on lost railroad tracks

How many replicas of Woody Guthrie with cracked guitars
How many photocopies of longhaired Joan
How many Ginsberg facsimiles and carbon-copy Keseys
still wandering the streets of America
in old tennis shoes and backpacks
or driving beat-up school buses
with destination-signs reading 'Further'
How many Buddhist Catholics how many cantors
chanting the Great Paramita Sutra
on the Lower East Side
How many Whole Earth Catalogs
lost in out-houses on New Mexico communes
How many Punk Rockers waving swastikas?
Franco is dead but so is Picasso
Chaplin is dead but I'd wear his bowler
having outlived all our myths but his
the myth of the pure subjective
the Little Man in each of us
waiting with Charlot or Pozzo
On every corner I see them
hidden inside their tight clean clothes
Their hats are not derbys they have no canes
but we know them
we have always
waited with them
They turn and hitch their pants
and walk away from us
down the darkening road
in the great American night

i was on my way to usc to do a talking piece and i had in mind to talk about language and money the two currencies and how solid they look how real and how however much they change they seem to be always the same solid like a greek coin or a nickel but when i got there the kids took me on the way to the auditorium through a trophy room filled with old cups and statuettes of little football players and baseball players running backs with those 1920s leather helmets worn by red grange and there in one case was the heisman trophy with a little golden running back on it threading his way through some broken field of the imagination and the last man i remembered getting one was o.j.simpson also from usc the great running back of the buffalo bills who does the tv commercial for hertz rent-a-car in which he threads through the main los angeles airport terminal like a runner on a punt return and winds up by jumping into his rented hertz "the superstar in rent-a-car" and this the trophy room the old fashioned football helmet reminded me of my childhood of football and baseball and stickball and my coming to california and running on the beach my sprained ankle the first shock of age and the way down our crumbling old house on the bluff over the water which took me

to real estate

david antin

while i do believe that what im doing essentially depends upon the event here going here and coming here and making what my idea of what a poem is or making my idea of what a valuable talk is if thats what poetry is on the other hand there is a life problem a kind of running down of ones life i may not be facing it very gravely now although actually when i came to california i started running on the beaches they have beaches and you can run on them and i twisted my ankle while running on the beach and it took a damned long time for my ankle to heal and having played football and baseball at various times in my childhood i always healed very quickly and this was the damnably longest healing that ever happened to me and i had an image of myself as a 40 year old pitcher which is not an easy thing to be forty year old pitchers have to watch where they put their feet and watch how they move and be careful that the mound is the right height because if they step off too fast they can lose it all that year and it was then i realized that life is running out somehow i didnt feel grave about it but somehow i had to be careful where i put my foot and id never had to be careful where i put my foot before see up to then i could just put my foot down and if it slammed against the pavement it didnt much matter if there was some pain it would be over the next minute or day and if i got knocked down by something i could get up again but i was beginning to realize that as with a car there is a limit on how long it can do it and so i had the feeling that in these pieces where i go out and talk its true that i regard the pieces as the center yet i still feel that because its running out and i dont have time to go all over to do the pieces all over the world im not omnipresent in all places talking to all the people i feel might benefit from hearing me talk or that i might want to talk to because i kind of enjoy the idea of talking to people i suppose i thought well ill put these things in books books are not ideal i dont believe that books are ideal forms that is books are imperfect recordings of transactions that occur in real time im here now and im trying to make a piece the way artists have probably always tried to make real work once and at some point ill take an imperfect record of what ive done and it will be an imperfect record because it will only be on acoustical tape and it will only get some of the effect of being here because what i say to some degree is determined by what you think or my sense of it otherwise id have to do an entirely separate berkleyian ego trip where i would talk about anything independently of who i think you are this is not my approach to poetry i suspect that the approach to poetry of poets in their natural habitat which is in performance and in performance improvisation has always been a response to some very specific set of urgencies that is homer told the story that way that time we have only two of those tellings reworked several times probably but we only have two of them who knows why he decided to tell all about odysseuses son telemachus for some reason something tripped him out on telemachus while he was taking up odysseuses return that day at that place maybe he was at a place where it was important that he should talk about the island where telemachus went to get advice from an old man maybe some relative of the old man was in the audience someone who was in the family line maybe somebodys son was there and his father was gone and homer knew it there is no reason to suppose that these things were done so that there could be comparative literature 134 in which you take up the odyssey and the iliad as the two great surviving works of all time its hard to believe that he was looking forward to an infinite posterity preparing your grim tasks to worry about a greek aristocracy that had long since vanished it seems unlikely it seems more likely that he had something to say and that the stories were familiar but the way he told them was dependent on some set of accidents like there being these people here and still there is the book homer need have had no respect for books i doubt if homer would have cared about ever being translated by robert fitzgerald say and i think robert fitzgerald knows that too i would by no means want to suggest that robert fitzgerald is under any illusions that he was doing something for homer i dont think homer would have cared but we now feel a certain anxiety about being locked in being in a small room dying in a small room as it were without telling someone outside the room what the room was like maybe because its valuable to know what its like in this small room maybe something happened valuably in this small room i dont believe that everything has to be sent everywhere i dont believe in globalism im not a globalist which is why i dont speak with a rhodes scholar accent or part of the reason in my university there are many people who have strange accents that when im stuck with committee meetings i normally try to analyze phonemically and they have very strange phonetic structures because they were exchange students somewhere in england occasionally and i recognize iowa under cambridge and i keep saying that sounds like iowa but then it sounds like cambridge and then it sounds like a fantasy of cambridge and i cant quite get it and then theres a little bit of la jolla mixed in it becomes an interesting task to dissociate the parts of this accent that are a consequence of a belief in some kind of generally globally appropriate style now the book itself can be considered a package a kind of care package so to speak right i mean i do my talking here and i take my imperfect recording and i transcribe it in the hope of finding what in it was the real thing the real action and i try to get it into the book in such a way that its still intelligible when it goes into this rectangular object with covers that you turn like this and which is partitioned arbitrarily by those things they call pages there are no pages when i talk you dont turn anything at all that is i turn you turn but we dont turn pages someone doesnt bring down a screen in front of me every few minutes and then let me continue again now the book has this problem but then everything has this problem that is talking also has its inherent difficulties there is no such thing as a perfect medium thats why they call it a medium because its in the middle so to speak its between it mediates a transaction and deflects it you start out to reach for something thats under water and your hand goes to the wrong place and after a while you realize that the object under the water is differently situated from you than you would have imagined it to be if it were outside the water and under the air let us say because water has a different relation to light rays than air which you dont really think about and are good at reaching through because thats what you are almost always seeing and reaching through so that under air you almost always find it because thats the way you learned about seeing and reaching whereas under water its really not where you think it is because thats where it would be under air and its really not there but then you reach again and you find it after a number of tries and you realize that the water is a medium as the air is a medium and the lens of your eye is a medium well language is also a medium that were talking through that is maybe there isnt anything but the language when we think finally but theres some sense in which we feel ourselves moving toward the language toward the language to go through the language and the language has its habits its specific density its index of refraction and i can use the habits of the language if i know what im doing with them and sometimes i get used to them and i get very expert and i forget theres going to be a crack in the grain somewhere over there and im going to get stuck with something something i dont want because it is the habit of the language to divide the world that way in that zone and its not my inclination to divide the world in quite that way and then ive got trouble poets have always had trouble with language anyone who uses it seriously has trouble with it it goes the way it wants to go because of the way people took it before and im a foreigner in it youre a foreigner in it do you realize its the one thing we all are is that were all foreigners in the language you know its very funny to talk about acquisitions of secondary languages because nobody comes in speaking the language you come into the world not speaking it and its their language and theyve spoken it and you havent spoken anything youve been involved in looking in feeling and touching in transactions with them and all the while they keep talking this foreign language and gradually you take it from them and you get to think of it what you get to think of it you may be suspicious of the way they use language maybe you think that theyre saying strange things that you dont agree with but in order to get them to do nice things to behave reasonably you pretend to accept their language and after a while youve accepted enough of it to be called a "native speaker" which is itself a lie of the language in a real sense there is something of a lie in this there is no such thing as a "native speaker" "native" would suggest that there is such a thing as someone who was born speaking it there is no such person who was born speaking it we are all born foreigners and its very important to remember that were all foreigners and all languages are secondary to our being because before that there were

meaningful transactions and we all got involved in them   i dont
know what it is to be before the language   but what i know now is
that the term "native speaker" has come to seem alien to me again
because "native" doesnt seem to go with "speaker"   it seems
to be an odd juxtaposition of two terms that are somewhat at odds with
each other   an exaggeration of a sort   an overoptimistic one
that promotes a false union   that somehow because were all here
now and seem to be at home here and seem to have been at home here as
long as we can remember   speaking a common language that we all
understand   it would seem as though we were born here speaking one
language and we all share a native currency   could you imagine
having a "native currency"   coming into the country with its money
being born with a supply of its money   is it really that
different   to be born with dollar bills in your pocket   not in
your parents pocket but in your pocket   but then you dont have pockets
and thats not trivial   you dont have pockets and you dont have
dollar bills in them   look   take a dollar bill   heres a
dollar bill   see it doesnt mean very much at this point   but its
wonderfully formalized   the dollar bill has all the great marks of
our unity together on it   it has the numeral one printed in all four
corners and on both sides   it has the founding father of our
country in the center of it   our first president   number one and
on the other side   the reverse side   his place is taken by the
word ONE   which in case you are in any doubt about it is also
printed over each of the numeral ones in the four corners of that same
side   and it is wonderful in its promise of a beginning   a new
order of centuries   from out of the many one   beginning with
one   and it is all very wonderful   as it states unequivocally
that this is legal tender for all debts public and private   and you
may believe this   i used to believe it too   i used to believe
it too i was an artist in residence at notre dame   which is a funny
place to be an artist in residence   i kept thinking ill be an
artist in residence and ill be talking to the football team   which
was kind of nostalgic for me   but i got there and they had me in this
funny motel   notre dame had a great motel   theyre terrific on
motels because all the tractor salesmen from duluth come down on
saturday to watch the football games   so they make a lot of money on
the motel   and i was in the motel and i thought   well what i
ought to do is rent a car   because on the weekend   if you dont want
to go to the ballgame   which i didnt really   you might want to
go see some other part of the country   and i came provided with a
fair supply of dollar bills and i went to call the car rental agency
o.j.simpsons company?   it was one of those companys   that
this guy goes running to a car and makes a mad leap to get into it
because he has no time for formalities or something or other
o.j.simpson the man with the heisman trophy out there in the hall
went running to this car   but presumably he didnt go there waving
dollar bills   because if he went there waving dollar bills they
would have said go away   o.j.simpson doesnt wave dollar bills he
waves credit cards   i found very fast that i could wave all the
dollar bills i wanted to   they wouldnt rent me the car   it says
here   and i read it to them   i took my dollar bill out of my
pocket and i read "this note is legal tender for all debts public and
private"   i said how much do you want?   ill rent your car ill
pay you in advance   ill give you a deposit   they said havent
you a credit card from some major company   i said not only do i have
a credit card from some major company i have a credit card from the
most major company in the united states   the united states
because basically thats what the country is its a credit card
company   its a credit card company and these are the credit cards
they said no   we dont accept those   i said you must be

unamerican i said its the biggest credit card company in the united
states   because it is the united states it prints all this money
they said we dont take it   so all week long i couldnt get away
from notre dame   except when driven by friendly students but
i had no way of moving out on my own because they didnt accept
dollar bills   which as i understood it were legal tender   but
they were not legal tender as far as car rental companies went they
would not accept payment they would not accept deposits they didnt
accept these green things   and i said to myself all these years
i used to think this was money   and i had an image of money
you know   i didnt think a lot about money   i confess
as a kid i didnt really think much about money at all   but
money was a kind of solid to me when i was a kid   because
well because of the way its presented   you know some of its
even very pretty   we used to have nickels that had the head of a
very beautiful indian on one side   and a buffalo on the other
these two vanishing species   and they both looked
wonderful   and i used to look with admiration at my nickel i
really liked my nickels   i was a little kid   jefferson on this
one doesnt really look very good   but i dont have any buffalo
nickels left   if you do theyre probably worth more than nickels
which goes to show you that if money is worth a lot of money
it goes out of circulation   which i believe is called greshams
law   that cheap money drives expensive money out of existence
the law meaning that whats cheesy stays in existence and whats not
cheesy you pull away from transactions because you dont want to give it
up   and i liked nickels   i really did   not only because of
what they could buy   i thought the nickels were really very nice
i had a jar full of buffalo nickels   the different years of buffalo
nickels   they went on for a while and i think they pulled them out
of circulation   some time after the second world war buffalo nickels
vanished and buffalo nickels and indian head nickels became extinct
and only were kept in peoples private collections   but these
nickels were very tangible to me   if you took a nickel down to a
grocery store   you could buy two coconut-covered marshmallow
candies   if thats what you liked and at that point i did
if you took one nickel to the candy store you could trade it for a
spaldeen rubber ball   with which you could play stickball
which was very nice because we played a lot of stickball and the
spaldeen was considered a very good ball   spaldeen was the name of
the ball   or we used to call them spaldeens   though now that i
think of it they were probably spaldings   but in our neighborhood
and in our dialect we called them spaldeens   and these spaldeens
were very much admired because they were much livelier than other balls
we used to test them out when we bought them   because even
among spaldeens youd occasionally get a dead one   and we used
to test them out by dropping them from about shoulder height to make
sure that it would bounce chest high or at least over your waist
because if it only bounced knee high it was a dead one and then
nobody would be able to hit a home run   and youd wind up with
a kind of pitchers duel   even though you had no pitchers when
you played stickball   because stickball as we played it in the
streets of new york was played with a stick and a ball and the stick was
an old broom stick   what you used to do was saw off the end of the
broom   though i never saw anybody saw it off everybody always seemed
to have one   really they always had these sticks and nobody ever
sawed them off at all   somehow they grew sawed off   and we
used to go into the street with our stick and our spaldeen and play
stickball   which was a game like baseball   except that you
threw the ball up in the air and you hit it on the first bounce
which is why you used to be concerned for the ball not to be dead

and usually you stood with your stick at home plate which was one of those sewer lids actually entrances to the gas and electrical lines that ran under the citys streets and placed at about 30 yard intervals so you had the batter standing over one sewer lid that was home plate and you played with first second and third basemen no shortstop because the streets were so narrow and usually one or two outfielders and in order to give the outfielders room because the streets in brooklyn were so narrow you usually played up near the end of the street with second base the sewer lid nearest the end of the street so that the outfield could play in the "T" of the intersection and you used to count sewer lids to describe the quality of your hitters and if you were a two sewer hitter you were really very good because you could hit the ball on the fly across cortelyou road which was the name of the broad avenue that intersected with east fourth street where we played and if you were a two sewer hitter you could hit it over the head of the one or two outfielders who patrolled cortelyou road and if you were lucky it would sail over their heads and if they were lucky they didnt get hit by the bus that traveled up and down the avenue you had to be very alert as an outfielder because you had to field the ball between the buses because cortelyou road was a fairly heavily traveled street even in the days before the smog hit because it was a big street that took you down to the major local shopping area on flatbush avenue the others were very narrow little streets and cars came about every half hour so you didnt have to worry about them and thats what i used to think was the average rate for cars to come through places about once a half hour you would see a car and you got through a lot of innings and when a car would come everybodyd walk to the side of the street and the car would sort of drift through at about ten miles an hour and youd go back to playing stickball now in those days i thought of money as real because the prices of things were constant in my experience they were fairly constant anyway little hooton chocolate bars were two cents coconut-covered marshmallows were about that price yoyos were a nickel spaldeens were a nickel tops were a nickel this may begin to sound like a nostalgia trip but you see everything in my world it was a childs world was fairly stable the price structure was stabilized and these things that you wanted and used were all objects and these things that were money were objects too a nickel a yoyo a spaldeen five pennies two marshmallow candies one top two hooton bars and you could trade them for each other in regular exchanges five pennies for a nickel or a top or a spaldeen the same way you could trade the spaldeen for a yoyo or a top or two marshmallow candies or a coke or a big puree shooter and it was clear this was money now in my family there were people who probably didnt think that way about money they must have assumed that money was a unit in a capacity to build something that would end up by making more of itself they call that capital but never mind about that there is a threshold effect in piling up money you pile up enough of it to become contagious you eventually get together a lot of nickels and eventually they start reproducing themselves at a certain point i had no such experience of money and no such theory of money as an agent of infectious disease and i only knew money as a set of simple and desirable objects you could exchange for other objects of equivalent desirability and size like the ration tokens we used to get during the war little red ration tokens that were smaller than money and you needed them to get various things like meat or butter that you bought during the war because meat was rationed and butter was rationed things like that but there were people there in my family who were more disillusioned with money than i was at the time because to me money was like a brick a yoyo a kite and i thought i understood money in those days it cost me 11 cents to go to the movies on saturday which is ten cents or one dime or two nickels and a penny tax for kids to go to the movies on saturday and it seemed fair enough then it went to 22 cents when it went to 22 cents i just thought it cost more money that something had happened to the movie it didnt occur to me that something had happened to the dime i was not in a position to recognize that the dime had changed its character because the entire nature of a coinage is to deny that money changes its character it is very important to recognize that the beauty of money that the great engraving and designing skills normally employed in putting out money is part of a long tradition of making money look stable of making money look like a durable thing a nickel looks like a nickel for ever it may eventually not contribute to buying anything at all but it still looks like a nickel the dollar looks like a dollar though if the dollars appearance were related to its function it would have nearly disappeared by now having started at one size it would now be but a shred of itself but the image of it is unchanged now this image of the constancy of money is very much like the image of the constancy of a language it seems to me that there is a relationship between the solidity of money and the solidity of the language which is very similar the language is also a coinage its a coinage and its in circulation people accept it and people modify it but all the time people have the illusion that the coinage remains the same and that theyre talking the same language they have the illusion because the illusion is fostered by a kind of nationalism a nation you might say is an institution organized to stabilize credit language credit buying credit maybe its the same credit nationhood is invested in objectifying credit nationhood is a formal celebration of the objecthood of language and credit and what it attempts to do is to give the appearance of regularization to human transactions throughout the culture now all over the country people are buying and selling the same or seemingly identical things and services and notions at wildly varying prices while almost everyone is under the illusion that these transactions are more or less uniform throughout the culture because the national system of coinage and language has provided a way of picturing these wildly varying transactions that makes them look more or less uniform by framing them within the apparently regular dimensions of our coins or our words in a way that is most satisfactory to the people who manipulate them most efficiently now there were people in my family who could have told me though they never told me very much but they could have told me that this was not likely first of all i came from a family where everybody spoke several different languages which makes the situation look very unstable anyway they spoke russian and german and yiddish and french and so there we were in my household for me to listen to a conversation usually meant that i had to learn one other language because kids have very great suspicion that somebodys saying something that theyre not supposed to hear the fastest way to get kids to learn another language is to gossip in another language and its amazing how fast theyll pick it up because they dont want to be shut out from the gossip so i went through all this keeping up with my peoples languages and it was a lot of fun i enjoyed it all but that could have told me theres no telling where you might have to go or what language you might have to speak that is as long as you dont

have to go anywhere   and you always stand still   you never
have to talk any other language   because youre always in the same
place and everything stays pretty much the same   the nickel always
stays the nickel   wealth is always wealth   legal tender is the
same   all the meanings attributed to the coinage are the same up and
down the system   but   there were members of my family who
distrusted this   they didnt trust money at all   and there were
two passions they developed   passions for land and passions for
objects   you see there is something in the coinage of the language
called *real*   estate   you may laugh at the relation between
"real" and "estate"   but real means thingy estate   you know it is
that estate which is real   and doesnt go away   it doesnt go
away because it is like the earth   the earth stays   the money
well   whatever happens to the money happens to the money but
there was in this family a remote relative   and he had come the
hard way here   he had come from russia   after an abortive
revolution   in russia in 1905   in which hed made the mistake of
turning a printing press   he had turned this printing press which
had printed out in ukrainian various calls to arms and human dignity or
whatever   in the name of whatever he had called it   because its
not clear to me what they said   it seems to me that when the
revolutionaries went down to speak to the peasants of the ukraine
they did not make speeches to them about the rights the rights of
man   they said to them sometimes the tsar is angry at the landlords
for taking away the fruits from the lands of his people   weve had
enough of these scoundrelly landlords and what we need is land for the
peasants   the peasants who understood land very well and had no
special ideas about freedom responded rather well to this   and
gathered together to help the tsar rid himself of oppressive landlords
and then found themselves being attacked by the tsars soldiers for
having helped the tsar rid himself of these worthless landlords
something like that was probably in the manifestos that were being
spread down in the south   because as lenin said on some other
occasion   "liberty is bread"   *Khleb Svoboda?*   i dont know
it doesnt sound right to me   they seem a little different but
perhaps there is a relation   and he was calling attention to a
relation as if it were an equation   and it was an effective
analysis for the time   however it wasnt effective for my relation
who was promptly put in prison when the revolution was crushed with
guns and swords and many of the peasants killed and such of their
leaders and assistants as the tsars forces could find were put in jail
from which this relative   with the help of some money from his
friends and relations   was able to escape and disappear through the
latvian corridor   and he had to take his ukrainian russian german
yiddish out through latvia   get into whatever boat he could buy a
passage on and go somewhere   out of the tsars reach   which
usually meant going somewhere where there was another relative who had
gone before   so these refugees were likely to wind up in the
united states or in cuba or mexico   and this one wound up in
argentina   philip was his name   and there he was in
argentina   and where before this he knew about rubles there he was in
argentina dealing with argentine pesos and speaking no spanish   he
quickly learned enough spanish to work in a cigar factory   and there
he took his previous skills   which were odd skills   he was
something of an athlete   he was a wrestler greco roman style
which is a form of wrestling i dont know too much about   except
that its sufficiently different from most other kinds of wrestling that i
feel i should point out that he was a wrestler greco roman style
and he was now rolling cigars in argentina   while his brother
who had gotten out of russia through the latvian corridor at nearly

the same time   for some reason through some connection   they had
apparently collaborated in proving that bread was freedom   and this
brother had somehow wound up in the united states   where he had
settled in new york on second avenue   the brother was something of
an artist   he had a knack for a kind of witty caricature like
painting and whimsical wood carvings   and this brother continued
his politicizing for the peasants   he had come to the united states
where there were no peasants   but there were workers   the
distinction between peasants and workers is fairly considerable for
marxist theory   which distinguishes between them rather precisely
but in revolutionary practice whoever is ready to revolt becomes a
revolutionary force   and philips artist brother was familiar with the
adjustment of theory to practice   so that on second avenue he
contributed his revolutionary cartoons appropriately enough   to a
newspaper called _die freiheit_   freedom   which was concerned
with liberating the workers of the garment district or the furriers
trade from the bonds and thralls of the sweatshops in a somewhat
similar manner to the way he had previously contributed them to the
cause of land reform   and philips brother   who was a very witty
caricaturist   received a certain amount of recognition and acclaim
as a newspaper artist   and he even made a certain amount of money at
it   so he wrote to philip in argentina   who was meanwhile
working in a cigar factory   where he was acquiring a whole new set
of skills and understandings   because in latin american cigar
factories they did not have that totally contemptuous relationship
to the people who worked there   or rather the people who worked in
these factories did not have a totally contemptuous relationship to
themselves   and to counteract the boredom of rolling and packing
cigars they ordinarily selected one of their number who happened to
have a particularly attractive reading voice to read aloud to them while
they worked   so they would have read to them   cervantes and lope
de vega and calderon and quevedo   and most of what were considered
the masterpieces of the spanish language   along with whatever
serious modern works fell into their hands and seemed appropriate for
reading aloud   so that after they had been there a while they had
heard most of the classical literature of spain and argentina in this
cigar factory   where philip was becoming very literate   in
spanish   but not wealthy   when he received a ticket to the
united states   where there was the possibility of becoming wealthy
but in english   which he didnt know   fortunately for him on
second avenue when he arrived there   there were many other people who
though they didnt speak spanish or even russian   spoke the
lingua franca of most jewish emigres from middle europe   yiddish
now yiddish is basically a rhineland germanic language that
predates standard german   being a dialect that was formed in the
rhineland in the middle ages by speakers who appear to have emigrated
from romance language speaking countries   parts of what we now
think of as france and spain   and this dialect as it spread with its
community of speakers was populated by hebrew words and then slavic
and eventually technical terms from german and whatever else that
allowed it to serve as this common coinage   and philip spoke this
language   as he also spoke russian and polish and ukrainian   and
now spanish as well   but with the particular idiosyncrasy and
inflection of his background and experience   which is typical of
a lingua franca   which is a common coinage that is exchanged far and
wide over vast terrains by a loosely joined community of talkers who are
accustomed to making exchanges in several coinages besides the one they
may happen to be talking in   which sometimes leads to differences of
opinion about the equivalences of some of the coins they happen to be

exchanging   differences id often observed among my relatives when
they were talking   differences like the one between two relatives
one had been living in argentina while the other had been living
in the united states for many years   which didnt really impede
their conversation   because they were speaking in yiddish and not in
spanish or english   and there they were sitting in the living room
calmly talking till one of them   the american remembered something he
had forgotten to do and asked the other to wait a moment because he had
to go downstairs to attend to something in his store   only it
happened that he said "store" as if it was a word of yiddish
ikh muss arunter ins store (i have to go down to the store)
the other was puzzled *vos eysst a "stor"* (what's a store?)
(where you do business) *vo muh treybt gesheft*   *ohh ir meynt a*
bodega (ohh you mean a *bodega*)   so that it was clear that in the
yiddish of the argentine you went down to your *bodega* while in the
yiddish of new york you went down to your *store*   and it was
situations like this that should have prepared them all these relations
of mine for shifting currencies   you would assume it   that they
would have been prepared to handle these currencies somewhat
skeptically   because they so often had to change them   but
these people who were so good at exchanging languages and currencies
didnt learn the whole lesson   they were so good at learning languages
they learned them so quickly that they quickly became natives
became natives with whatever funny accent they may have happened to
have   because some   though not all of them spoke each new
language with a slightly alien accent that was a part of the old system
of coinage they had so recently left   so they had whatever funny
accents they had but they were already feeling like native speakers of
english   because it is one of the main functions of speaking a
language at all   to make you feel like a native and to make
whatever way you speak it seem natural and stable   as it is also to
make every other way of speaking it strange and everyone who speaks it
strangely some sort of foreigner   and these new natives of english
these relatives of mine soon felt very good in english and at home
in it as they spoke it   but they still had some distrust of their
countrys printed currency   to the extent that they sensed that if
they kept on accumulating this currency for any length of time its
buying power might suddenly diminish or be extinguished   and to the
extent they sensed this they looked about for other things they could
exchange their money for that were in some way more valuable   more
durable   more real than money and this astute greco roman wrestler
cigar roller   with the classical spanish education   that he
had acquired in the cigar factory   came to new yorks second avenue
and found employment in the fur business   i think   and managed to
make a fair amount of money   in fact considerably more money than
his artist brother   and because he had reasonably frugal habits and
nothing in particular to spend this money on he soon acquired a small
pile of this money   and was soon looking about for things that
were realer than this money to exchange it for   for some way of
realizing this money   making it more real than legal tender   and
he had a passion for the open air for greenery   for nature
and this was a passion he shared with many of the people living in
the grey   brick buildings of second avenue   and the artist and
intellectual world he traveled at the fringes of   because he was not
an artist and he didnt seem to them to be an intellectual either   he
was a relatively taciturn man who didnt speak much to the others about
art or politics or spanish literature even   and was thought to be
something of a fool   but he was a shrewd man and parsimonious
the kind of man dollars stick to   or pesos or rubles   and

as he saved his money he observed that all of these urban artists and intellectuals in their grey city had a dream of nature   of things green and fresh and flowering   and they found their way somehow to this nature   up the hudson on the old routes 9W and 17   north past the big apple rest   over the ferry at newburgh or through nyack   to a part of nature called sullivan county   which was a somewhat depleted form of the nature it had once been   an oak and beech and chestnut forest mingled with spruce and hemlock   and it had been logged out for the lumber and then for tanbark   and had then gone to farming   with apple orchards and dairy farms   and among these failing farms   they had found their way to these small things called bungalows   bungalow   i once read a poem by paul eluard where he said that he would never use the word bungalow in a poem   i never thought i would use the word bungalow in a poem either but here it is   what they used to call a bungalow was a flimsy wooden shack where too many people camped cheerfully out of a love of nature surrounded by a number of other such shacks at the edge of a bit of scrub forest   and they found these bungalow colonies   where people could commune immediately and directly with nature   at the edge of this scrub forest   in these little places with kitchens and bedrooms with screens over the windows called bungalows   now philip   who made his way up here and observed the pleasure it gave those people to be out in the open air   quickly saw the value of these bungalows   which were fairly simple to build and since he was as skillful with his hands as at acquiring money he soon exchanged some of his money for land on which he soon built a number of these bungalows   and soon he sold bungalows   because he had a grander view than bungalows   and as these bungalows became more expensive   more valuable in exchange   he exchanged these bungalows for land   and more land   lots of land   not many people wanted this land because nobody could live there in this wasted beech woods and evergreen forest   you see it was real estate all right   the estate was real   there were trees and there were frogs   and there were birds in the trees and there were streams that ran beside the trees   but nobody could live there in this wasted beech and evergreen woods that had been logged out   and where farming was unprofitable because the distances you would have to transport your products to a reasonable market were too great and the cost uneconomical   so that only very large dairy farms or chicken farms could afford to transport their milk or their eggs to a market and come out ahead   given the relative costs of feed and fuel and milk and eggs   so that most of the small farms were gradually abandoned when the old farmers died and their children had gone off to the city to live   which is why this was nature because nobody could live there   they could only vacation and so philip bought acres and acres of this land   and on it he and his artist brother began to build   and what did they build there they built   a swiss chalet   because thats how nature should look   nature should surround these beautiful half timbered rough hewn buildings with great halls   and they built a great halled swiss chalet in which the beam ends were carved by the artist brother and in which the artist colony of lower new york came to vacation and this great hall which was the hotel dining room was inscribed with liberating slogans   freedom through joy   pleasure is knowledge   desire the open   and the like   and besides this on the walls of the dining room the artist brother painted a series of energetic caricatures depicting in a dire way the vices of refusing this liberation and their hilarious personal consequences   and people came and the place developed a kind of   cultural dominion   in western sullivan county   concert pianists came there to play roving and unemployed violinists of consummate skills   folk singers actors from the classical yiddish theater and there too came chess players debaters artists and art lovers and professionals and various socialist workers and bosses the intelligentsia now this would never have happened in this way except for marriage because one brother was able to build and the other was able to decorate but nobody was able to manage that is nobody was able to deal effectively with money as capital because while philip could save what he mainly knew was that land was real wood was real and money well he didnt trust it too much and the artist brother wasnt interested in money either he was interested in a life of art and talk and girls and food in the midst of nature which gave the place its tone of a socialist intellectual nudist colony up there in western sullivan county now it happened that the artist brother in the course of things had an affair with one of the young women who were attracted to this good life up there and this particular young woman was not only an attractive woman but she was also a very clever young woman and very much attracted to the liveliness and beauty of the place so that this affair lasted a good deal longer than most of the affairs of the artist brother who was something of a one-upman in sexual matters and could never stay with anyone long once she had become familiar and no longer an object of possible romantic intrigue so that in a way im not entirely sure about he finally rejected her like all of the others but since she was probably as much attracted to the place as to the man she never stopped coming and she turned to the other brother who was greatly surprised as you might imagine no woman had ever looked upon him with passion or interest unless he had moved in their direction first he was not a conventionally attractive man though he had a noble head with a craggy dramatic face and the powerful body of the athlete he had been but he was very broad and thick and short like a chunky guard on a professional football team though he was maybe a little short for a guard and what he looked like most was a small bear and in spite of his considerable classical spanish education and his russian and german social political and economic education and his proven ability to make money he was thought to be dumb perhaps this was because he never spoke much about these things and when he did he spoke very slowly and with great deliberation because he thought while he was speaking and seemed to be making a great effort to say no more and no less than he meant so that he often had to slow down phrases and words while he was in the middle of them which resulted in strange distortions of emphasis and pronunciation that people found laughable or exasperating while they waited for him to get on with the conversation so they thought he was dumb and he knew that they thought so but this young woman somehow managed to convey to him beyond his suspicions natural as they were that she was interested in him and they got married at which point she lost her interest in him immediately but she remained interested in the place which she helped to build up in a way that was beyond their expectations because she was even more clever than she was attractive and because she was attractive she helped attract a male clientele and among that clientele there was one quite wealthy man a sweater manufacturer with whom she contracted a long liaison and because she was clever with his help she managed to borrow money which she quickly invested in buildings with rooms and more rooms in which they could put more and more of these cultured people who came to vacation in the midst of this nature now these buildings were not swiss chalets or were only superficially decorated to look like swiss chalets because this young woman had no particular image of how this nature should look but she had a particularly good image of money and how to use it to make much more of it   and unlike the brothers she knew how to borrow it and when and she knew how to use it and when to stop   so that under her management the place became much more prosperous and more and more of those people came to sit in their casino or dance in it   talk in their dining halls   and walk in their woods   while their children swam in the swimming pool and played on the tennis courts and these people all regarded themselves as what is called the <u>intelligentsia</u>   people like rosa schiller   who was a doctor whod emigrated from austria with her husband   also a doctor and with her sister who lived with a small dog in an overstuffed apartment   overlooking central park south   and who was now in her sixties and still in her own eyes and in the eyes of her 70 year old beaus an international beauty   while rosa lived the intellectual life with her husband in elizabeth new jersey   where they had adjoining offices   and conducted their separate practices but emerged into a common central room   a library filled with leather volumes where they took lunch together and read the agamemnon to each other in greek   and i had seen this office   which was in their house fronted by a greenhouse and filled with rubber plants   and her ancient black and gold instruments   that might have been owned by breuer or freud   and i could imagine her and her long dead husband working all morning long and then rushing into this central study to read their greek plays and then hurrying back to treat some sore throats or   examine failing eyes   and the place was filled with people of this type   and this situation went on from year to year till the end of the second world war   after the second world war a great change took place socially   what exactly it was no one was clear about   but all of the people who came up there were getting older   some of the older ones died and the younger ones got older and there were fewer and fewer new ones to replace the ones that disappeared   because the ones who were children there   now that they were grown never came there   first of all because they didnt speak the european languages that gave the place a lot of its charm   and second they had no great interest in spending their time with their elders in a place where they had been children and had had counselors and where they knew every crack in the tennis courts and every leak in the porch roof   and very few new ones ever heard about this place in sullivan county where you could hear lectures on sholem aleichem in the morning discuss emma goldman or rosa luxemburg at lunch   hear chopin ballades in the evening and dance the alexandrovsky or the russian two step late into the night   because the reservoir from which they drew these people was also disappearing as second avenue had dispersed to great neck   and new brunswick and new rochelle   and though this happened gradually   the number of people coming up gradually diminished and the place became less and less profitable at one point it had been very profitable   which is not to say that it had always been filled   because hotels in nature were filled only part of the time   but every weekend it had been filled to overflowing   and about half of the summer   and the rest of the time there had still been enough people left to give the sense and provide the income for a thriving business   and now less and less of the summer was filled   and filled got to mean something different because none of the outer buildings was ever jammed to capacity anymore and they never had to pitch tents on the lawn to handle the overflow   and the business which had been very profitable became less and less profitable   but the buildings didnt go away   you see   once youve got buildings theyre real   youve got buildings the buildings are real   youve got tennis courts the tennis courts dont go away   grass grows up in them   you still have to chlorinate the pool   youve got to repair the roof after each winter and repaint the trim   and the buildings   they dont go away   but the people   may not be there anymore   and this continues for a period of time   and it comes on bad days and eventually the struggle to keep the hotel alive just wore them out   and the young woman   who was now no longer a young woman but still clever didnt really understand this and had taken to drinking   she drank champagne all day and all night   and the artist brother   feeling depressed because this place had been his culture center   because he had made almost all of his art works there and there they were on the walls of this place that was dying   this artist brother sickened and died   and there was a grand funeral for him to which all of the writers and artists who had once gathered on second avenue came   and hundreds of people came to this funeral and to a final exhibition of his art that was arranged in a gallery to pay homage to all the years of his work   and he was buried   so the intellectual center disappeared   and just at this point philips wife became sick   and some people said it was because the artist brother had died and she had been conducting an affair with him all these years and now that he was dead there was nothing in it for her anymore   and she became something of an invalid and no longer took any interest in the place   and it continued to run down   except for philips working on the place constantly   keeping up the buildings repairing them because he believed in the physical place   the buildings and the land   it seemed everything he had he threw into the physical plant   he had always made money easily and he had made a lot of it from the place   so he put great quantities of it back into the place from which he had gotten it   and in spite of the fact that it kept running down it was extraordinarily beautiful   in this western corner of sullivan county right near the delaware river there was this strange european set of chalet-like buildings   to which fewer and fewer people came   though any new ones who came there found it   exotic and colorful   as i found it when i had occasion to work there one summer as a lifeguard   and you could always find someone who had played chess with lasker sitting on the porch looking over endings or hear a russian court dance float down through the spruce trees to the library where you were playing poker with the concert pianist and a few of the waiters   now it happened that at about this time my wifes mother became the manager of the place   at the time when it was declining but still beautiful   and at first it was a job   as it had been when she was a waitress there in the time of its fading glory while philips brother and philips wife were still alive   and she had been an assistant manager as it continued to fade   and on the death of philips wife she became the manager   and this job became something more than a job   it became a passionate struggle to keep the place alive and restore it to its former dignity and affluence in the teeth of great changes socially that you couldnt stem   it was going downhill all the way   and philip encouraged her in this struggle   he encouraged her somewhat financially   by lending her bits of money to invest in the place and keep it up   but even more by giving her the impression that he would finally bequeathe it to her   because she also had a love for the place   for the idea of the place as an institution   as a look   while he had a love for the place as a physical tangible thing and he wanted it to be in the hands of someone who would take care of it and maintain it as that thing that he had known and loved   so he kept sending out signals to her that shed eventually acquire the place if she would only take adequate care of it   in the meantime there were

heirs who would normally have inherited the place   in the beginning
hed had a son who would have gotten it   but the son died suddenly
and mysteriously far away   even while philips wife was still alive
and then there was a sister who should ordinarily have gotten the
place except that she couldnt keep it up and the place was in debt
in terms of money there was no value to the property   the place
had used it all up and was not only not returning money to the people
who had put it in but was now taking more money away from them   the
property had become a kind of pump that was working in reverse   once
when it had been set in motion by the physical energy of its owners
or the stored energy of their money   it had pumped money out of
the hands of the people who were its customers into the hands of the
people who were its owners   but now it was pumping money steadily
out of the hands of its owners into the hands of its creditors   and
the people who ran it had to sustain it with more and more money
so that if you got this property what you got was a debt   and
a mortgage   with a second mortgage   in a bank   and that meant
that this place   real as it was   swiss chalet in the tall spruce
trees   was a debt owed to two banks in monticello   but none of
them looked at it that way   and in spite of the debt there was
in the family a great concern over who would get the place after
philip died   and philip was a long   time   living   and
the hotel was a long   time   losing money   each time assisted
to continue the next year   with loans from philip   who always
found a bit more money to put back into it   and always   just
about enough to keep it alive as a place   then   philip   died
when philip died various people who knew him   and were related
to him or his relatives were invited to the funeral   and philip was
about to be buried next to his wife bessie   these things are always
done in remote parts of long island   they are always buried in some
green place out in nature   where they have real estate   and
these places are way out there on the island   and they drove all the
way out to this place   after a moderately mournful funeral
moderate because he was an old man and a cantankerous figure and
not everybody loved him   and they all got out there   his sister
and his wifes brothers and the small crowd of close and not so close
relatives and a few friends   and they arrived at the place where
philip was to be laid in the grave next to bessie   and bessies grave
was evacuated   there was no bessie   cries went up from various
relatives "theyve dug up bessie!"   "what happened to bessie?"
in the course of the burial no one paid any attention to philip
because everyone was concerned with the missing bessie   bessie
was gone   gone bessie but the monument over the tomb   "here rests
the loyal husband and the loyal wife   true in death as they
were in life"   and no bessie   only philip   for weeks this
scandal was a great mystery   so great a mystery that most of the
relatives and acquaintances paid little attention to philips will
it went relatively unnoticed that he had bequeathed the worthless
hotel to his sister who was too old to run it   and trivial amounts
of money to various predictable relatives   while everyone was
astonished that nothing was said in it of the whereabouts of bessie
some people had theories   they said "well she didnt sleep with
him while he was alive   he didnt want her to sleep with him when he
was dead"   but nobody could find out   they went to the
cemetery people   the cemetery people checked their records and found
that in fact   philip had delegated someone to come and dig up bessie
but what had philip done with bessie   bessies relatives wanted
to find out where bessie had been sent   they searched and searched
something like a year later when philips sister was moving to a new

apartment she turned up by accident in a box of philips papers
which nobody had taken the trouble to look through he was not
an especially literate man except in spanish which they didnt know
she turned up a railway express ticket and they looked at this
railway express ticket and it had a number on it and they went and
tracked it down and the express people looked through their records
and they found that there had been some sort of large parcel
shipped to someone on the west coast someone in california
by railway express and that was all they knew with a
great deal of trouble the railway express people were persuaded to check
it out and after a while they found out that the parcel had in fact
been received by the express people on the west coast but
no one had came to call for it and theyd had no name of anyone to
whom to return it if it was not received after a lot of trouble
and time they found bessies coffin in a warehouse in fresno and
they restored it to the real estate that philip had been trying to
protect from her all of this time

THE ANONYMOUS / ANOMALOUS LETTERS OF PASSION

The Saga of S. Vireo

JAMES PURDY

In success as well as in misfortune no time is allowed for loitering.
S. Vireo, alias Puss Watermelon, alias Spotted Hen (his criminal nicknames would fill a city telephone directory), began his career when the patron who had been paying his bills for three years, F. Jeff Westlox, was fed to the teeth and threw him naked off the upper fire escape. He missed death by a fraction of an inch. He picked himself up, and being stark nude helped himself to what clothing was lying around in the garbage cans. He found a woman's wrapper, a man's poncho, and a cowpuncher's hat and shoes. None of the articles fitted him.

He went over (clothed in castoffs) and sat down on the curb and boo-hooed for about an hour.

The well-known détraqué millionaire Tuttle Morgan was driving around Prince Street, Manhattan, at about that hour of the day looking for new valets, and his chauffeur pointed out S. Vireo, more to amuse Tuttle Morgan than with the thought the derelict would be adopted (thereby perhaps crowding out the chauffeur, though S. Viero is an abominable driver and is said to have (while speeding on the turnpike) killed his grandmother and aunt).

"Would you care for a spin along the water?" Tuttle asked the Vireo.

"I don't have the choice of refusal," the Kentucky-born down-and-outer replied (or is said to have replied).

Now there were several factors in Vireo's former patron's having decided to throw him off the fire escape that hot June night. There was the scandal, you know, of the kangaroo meat dinner (unnatural feast).

But even before the kangaroo-raw-meat scandal there had been trouble between Vireo's F. Jeff Westlox and himself, as is evidenced by a letter which came into the possession of the police and which was written from Manhattan in the boiling summer heat when Vireo's patron was then enjoying the cool Nova Scotia breezes. It reads as follows (and is actually signed by Vireo):

PUSS VIREO'S STUDY: CHURCH SQUARE,
THE GREAT CITY

Master Jeff
Cooled Islands,
Nova Scotia, Canada

My former Dear:

I have been ill of compound migraine and the fact a mugger chained me to the roof in the broiling sun and then enjoyed my body over twelve times without genuine cessation or rest.

Now I am not writing you about my sufferings because I realize my sufferings should not taint your cool happiness when you are in the islands, but I do write in protest against your employing of detectives to spy on these sufferings, and the few joys connected with suffering itself. For that reason I somewhat (but not entirely) rejoice in the exposure of your purely sexual liaison with the criminal disguise-and-escape artist and coffee ventriloquist The Black-Crested Night Heron, wanted in 49 states for lewd posture and fraud, mayhem and murder.

I am sorry (naturally) that you have felt constrained to have bulldog and bloodhound agents hide behind my kitchen stove and refrig to ferret out (and jump out during) my few sex pleasures with routine partners of my election and hasty choice (my art keeps me from having the time to always choose wisely here for coital relief). My coital outlet is necessary owing to me being a migraine sufferer. I have to and must have steam-let-off in this fashion. As I say, there will be a lot of bread to be buttered when you return. As to your own peccadilloes which you like not to mention (guilt always makes you haughty), you will be lucky if The Black-Crested Night Heron lets you off without taking one of your own feathers away with him in custody. Remember he is no old sleep-possum, and once he gets a taste for somebody he goes on tasting that party. Regretting you have acted with such alacrity against me,

Your winter paramour,
Puss Vireo,
Church Square

The police got possession of another letter, and I as a former police stenographer and shorthand expert was loaned this letter also. It goes something as follows:

PRINCE PUSS VIREO HEADQUARTERS
Old Church Station,
Formerly Favorite to the Black Mama,
Now Private White Genius.

Master Jeff Westlox
The Cool Islands,
On the Larger Atlantic
Nova Scotia

Sir:

So you are accused, and I believe rightly, of being the lover of The Black-Crested Night Heron. I knew this would happen. You have been a haughty one, and have set the bloodhounds on me. Where are *my* bloodhounds? Under what lemon sky do I set these beasts on your guilty spoor? Under what sickle moon are my vampires biting?

Why have you been haughty and normal, when I am held under the paws of your bloodhounds? Mr. Butterfirm, your detective, has exposed me! I am naked unto moon and sun. I have no protective oil. I am known under aliases, all owing to your having sucked the feather of The Black-Crested Night Heron. I am guiltless, yet I am branded. My body is red from whips. You are guilty. You *would* go to the cool islands, leaving me sweltering. When I tried to gain a little cooling draft for my parched lips, although you were amid the feathers of The Black-Crested Night Heron, you begrudged me harmless caresses. You have everything, including cooling winds. I am branded and stung by big hornets on broiling roofs . . . Mr. Butterfirm be drawn and quartered (or halved by his ass). I will continue to yield my body to hot furred monsters. Since I am hot, let them hot me further. Mr. Butterfirm, know I am guilty because of my nostalgia! But I must have animal pressure because you have embarked with *your* pressures to the cool isles. Goodbye until I get my paws on you,

Signed (his paw) Puss Watermelon, White Genius[1]

The thing that broke the relationship between S. Vireo and his patron and paramour of several years, F. Jeff Westlox, was the cannibal feast of raw kangaroo meat, which unlike most such feasts was consummated at the wrong orifice. This took place after Vireo's meal ticket of that year, Jeff Westlox, returned from Nova Scotia.

Here is the news release which the police allowed me to see (they have over 8,000 such releases, which they keep and re-consult when there are unusual unsolved crimes going on.)

The Rover Mansion Lonely, Vermont
Special Press Release cv 874 XC 789
Immediate:
BLUE GRASS YOUTH ABDUCTED, TORTURED ON CANADA BORDER BY ECCENTRIC BILLIONAIRE ART PATRON: HIS OWN ROOMMATE FORCES HIM TO MALODOROUS FEEDING. HIS PRIVATE DIARIES FOUND, HEREWITH PRINTED.
Stephen Vireo's Notes Published Herewith:

Lonely, Vt., June 25. "I have been abducted, and forced to eat the hindquarters raw of the kangaroo!" These were the opening words of the Kentucky blue grass youth's private S.O.S. from the Rover mansion in Vermont, where he was abducted by his roommate, who "cuffed, lashed, scratched, and bit" him until he yielded to the eccentric Billionaire host in Rover and partook of raw kangaroo meat (at the moment of his gagging repast he was being given the "barbed wire" dig by his roommate . . .)

"When I could no longer eat the raw kangaroo meat (which was presented to me as the finest American Texas beef, knowing that I was partial to the kangaroo and could not bear its piteous cries when massacred) my roommate signaled to a German in the kitchen, and at another signal from him I was carried to a large spinning room of the mansion, denuded roughly (my roommate slapped me vigorously and gnawed my shoulder while I was being prepared for my ordeal), and my

[1] The well-known criminal, The Black-Crested Night Heron, was found mangled and garroted by steel piano wires in a dance hall on Orchard Street the next summer, after having himself received 82 anonymous letters all bearing the same message: "On second thought we will not use your fresh skull as a drinking cup owing to its fissures but we will employ it in a couple of weeks for incense burning. Signed Marshmallow Gutiérrez."

rectum was then completely uncovered and stretched with a large rubber ball-like instrument. When both my inner and outer rectum had been stretched to the point of bursting, fully three pounds of raw kangaroo meat were brought, I was slapped and spat upon, and the meat was stuffed into my rectum, both rectums, amid my cries, resembling the native kangaroo in peril, and my calling on my Mother to come to save me. My roommate slapped me again, and ordered another pound of raw meat brought.

"My host now entered in his surgical gown, and struck me. 'You'll learn the etiquette of being entertained by your betters, I hope,' he said, and he sprayed my face with his spittle. He inspected my rectum, and then shouted, 'He can hold another four pounds there!' After my ordeal I signed a paper, promising to eat everything put on my plate in the future, to praise the food, and especially its bloody rawness, to praise my host, my roommate, and renounce forever my individual hankering for my own ways . . ."

Mr. Vireo was carried back to New York on a wheeled stretcher. "You see, I have suffered. First at the hands of the Voodoo Queen La Mama, and now by the bloodstained paw of the murderer of that gentle creature the kangaroo . . . May that dear wild creature forgive me for having ingested his flesh . . . Allow me to weep, my sufferings are only now getting to my brain and it reports to me, 'You have known pure Atrocity, dear S.V., pure atrocity . . .' "

Special: Immediate.

There is one thing S. or Puss Vireo could not stand, and that was competition. He felt he was destined to be the only street performer in Manhattan of this period, and his having been thrown naked from a fire escape by his patron initiated him into a career as curb-and-street mime and acrobat from thence forward.

But the police for a short time (dating also from the hot summer of 1973) became interested in the infamous and of course beautiful Thespian Terence Clark, who possessed along with the greatest acting talent since Duse the power of weeping large fat tears at will. (He himself had been trained by a criminal prestidigitator and practicer of both black and white magic.)

I quote again from the police files (actually Terence Clark was never a threat to the prominence of Mime Vireo, but I want the reader to know about the Lachrymatory Laboratory just the same.)

THE LACHRYMATORY LABORATORY, LTD.,
Manufactury of Real and Artificial Tears,
Perfumes, Glycerine Concoctions, and
Attar of Roses from the White Rose Only.

Gutiérrez Blanco-Caballo, Manager

September, after the Equinox, 1974.

To: Terence Clark, Thespian,
The Great City

Dear Mr. Clark:

We have been creditably informed that you have been endowed from birth with the faculty of shedding tears at the drop of a pin. You may not realize the value of such an endowment owing to your rural origin and the fact you are an obscure actor. No other living creature, however, except the African Crocodile, has the gift which you are said to possess. In other words you are as valuable as a Crocodile.

As you know, I am the greatest, indeed the only Manufacturer and Bottler of Genuine and Artificial Tears. Crowned heads, great women of every walk of life, crowd my Laboratory. And if your own Mentors, the Cherokee Red Indian and the Owner of the Brooklyn Branding Parlors are to be believed, you can be persuaded to rent out your Lachrymal Glands for, say, one half hour a week.

I can promise you 80 guineas for that semi-hour. Do you agree? Mind you, I am indifferent in a total sense to your other more well-advertised charms—such as your latissimus dorsi muscle and your unusually dimpled kneecaps. You have, in other words, no appeal to me beyond your Crocodile faculty of exciting your own Lachrymal Glands, and only your tears will be extracted from your body in my Laboratory.

You will be slapped vigorously on entering the Laboratory by my chief assistant, known familiarly as "Boxing Kangaroo," as we have no time here for Tchaikovsky music to "mood" you to gradual secretion of your glands.

Whatever you do, however, do *not* bring the Cherokee Red Indian or the Owner of the Brooklyn Branding Parlors with you, or any other patron or mentor of yours. (We will give at least two of your mentors a "finding fee" for having put us on the track of your endowment.) But remember, no observers here while you are engaged in manufacturing tears.

Your tears on extraction will be bottled and sold to the mistress of an unnamed African potentate.

Awaiting you in our professional guise, I am, yours faithfully,

Gutiérrez Blanco-Caballo, Manager
and International Chemist

The Search for a New Patron

Tuttle Morgan soon tired of S. Vireo, and the burden of shelling out so much money afflicted him grievously. (It is Tuttle Morgan, worth 4 billion in the late summer of 1974, who is said to have remarked in Trinity Church, Wall Street, "All rich men hate to part with even a penny that they feel is not immediately cranking out more coin.")

Of course, Tuttle Morgan did not throw S. Vireo from a fire escape naked to the curb, but got him off his back by securing him a position at Serendipity as a dancer.

While employed as *dancer extraordinary* in front of the kitchen and near the boiler room he also applied for the usual eleemosynary gratuities from billionaires. (A famous fortuneteller has said that S. Vireo actually could [in the ridiculous jargon of the present era] "relate" only to billionaires. He despised Madame Wenderholt for instance because she was that pitiable thing 3 millions.)

Ferdinand Logan was 89 and worth 4 billion when last censused. He had seen a photo of S. Vireo dancing at Serendipity, and allowed he would consider the usual S.O.S. letter demanding pecuniary assistance owing to the Garbage Mime's having in the words of one of the more red-winged Foundations "indubitable, if loathesome talent."

However, Logan's heirs did not see it Vireo's way. They wrote:

FERDINAND LOGAN, HEIR,
The City,
The Gonzalez-Martin Suite
Cable GOOZE

Dear Sir:

Mr. Ferdinand Logan, Heir, has received your peremptory and entirely improper appeal for money for you to make indecent movies.

Although we usually inform the authorities when we receive demands for payment from unknown parties, Mr. Logan, the Heir, was willing to condescend and engage in this particular request. He has of course gone over your police blotter. Your blotter reads as follows:

> A delicate youth sometimes sallow after night excursions, delicate, but despite said delicacy incessantly engaged in the lewd doctrine movement. Recently sold his body in the Connecicut (sic) mountains. Is poor at arithmetic, and often doesn't charge his customers, or accepts mere gratuities. His mind somewhere else most of the time. Customers complain his flesh is bruised and cut, and this makes it difficult for him to charge full price for his favors. He has fogged-over eyes when he is cross, which is frequent.

Now to business. Mr. Ferdinand Logan has never cared a straw, fig, or partial plate for art, movies, books, theater or indeed humanity. His sole interest is making and keeping money and enjoying sexual company.

He has your pictures. His offer is frank and manly. He is willing to pay you for your sexual services. Where you put this money, on films, on you parading around in your bathrobe costumes or in banana peels is all one to him. However, owing to the confirmed rumor that your person is bruised and cut, and that you are often cross, and have foggy eyes, he would be able to pay you only 35 guineas an hour, during which of course you would submit to his total and undivided delectation. Remember, once you enter the Heir's apartments and chambers, you have no rights, no personality, and no will.

You need money, say it be for art or you parading around in your bathrobe and cornhusk costumes, well and good. But don't tell him about your hopes and aspirations. He hates them. Your bruised and cut body will be accepted for the nonce. Strike then the bargain while you are as free from bruises as the present, then go on with what he considers your ill-advised career.

Remember, this offer will not be repeated.

Should you make any untoward or illegal demands on Ferdinand Logan, he can and will turn your police blotter over to the Senate.

Yours, for Ferdinand Logan, Heir

Will F. Steffanson, Secretary,
and Officer-in-Residence.

During the tough winter, then, of 1975, Puss Vireo alias Watermelon alias Spotted Hen was watched closely by the police, and the Anonymous (or as some wisecrack called them Anomalous) Letters to Precinct 8** got bulkier.

The authorities knew of course Vireo was applying for financial aid from the wealthy lunatic fringe, such as the following letter attests to:

COUNTESS TALMA,
Suite 7, Empress Arcade
The City

Undated (owing to regulation 4387 C)

Dear Sir,

Your request for economic assistance and underwriting for you to make motion pictures of you dancing in ballrooms has been received by Countess Talma.

Countess Talma, however, is unable to assist you or your friend at this time.

Her "no" decision is based on two factors:

1) She is needful of more money herself, for jewels, gowns, and plume fans, and

2) According to the Federal Institute of Dangerous Youths, you are described thusly:

"Stephen Vireo is deemed by Private Eye 82 as a love burglar, and therefore perilous; he is a homewrecker, and bases his personality on the lewd doctrine school. He stars in his own costume films which are based on malodorous divagation, in part. He is a confessed paramour. Has been convicted twice as a blue-tape regular which is argot for anomalous passion. He is also trained in the western puff school of coarse passion, and unnatural address."

Under these circumstances Countess Talma must not be looked upon as one of your outlets, and under no future conditions should you appeal to her for amelioration of your situation which you describe as "lonely, awesome bad, and getting worse momently."

The Countess asks that you do not refer to her "no" communication. It will not be possible for her to recognize you socially as a result of your letter, and her reply.

For the Countess,

Guillaume Perecloche Gautier-Merz,
Secretary.

Vireo's notoriety as a garbage-costume-street performer also began to bring in money from unexpected quarters such as the following letter (Police File 8765 VV 9834):

EQUESTRIAN, LIMITED
SALVES FOR THE CELEBRITY &
THE DISTINGUISHED FEMME.
New City
The City

Dear Celebrity:

Your name has been suggested by a noted woman to EQUESTRIAN RECTAL PELLETS.

Would you allow your name to be used advertising this delicate palliative. You would say publicly in print the following:

STEPHEN VIREO, NOTED ART FILM MAKER:

"I have used EQUESTRIAN RECTAL PELLETS many times

while riding about movie studios and searching for new talent in the hills. They (the pellets) preclude fatigue, ease buttock weight, while a-horse, and soothe angry tissues—I mean *really* angry. My exacting work often makes me peevish and cross—that is why I consider EQUESTRIAN RECTAL PELLETS a must. I am never a-horse without them."

STEPHEN, ART FILM MAKER

You will be paid $18,000.00 for this testimonial. Please wire your decision to:

ESQUES. PELL
Grand Central Queen,
Box Queen #8 V
The City

About this time, success having gone to Vireo's head, he lost his sinecure as dancer extraordinary at Serendipity owing to his having in the words of the proprietor "lost all sense of decorum, proportion and Western decency." He was cashiered and dismissed by C. Zolt, and warned never to return.

Needing employment so bitterly, however, and having been turned down by the Lunatic Fringe Foundations such as Countess Talma, we turn again to our Police Blotter information for the next news of S. Vireo:

Mr. Zolt
Special to Inter-Continental and Atlantic World News Service, Immediate Release. Press Release 734 N 9 Z 876 C
Cable Inter via Hamburg
CHILD MIME-PANTOMIMIST VIREO TO KNEEL IN SNOW BEFORE SERENDIPITY IN BID FOR REINSTATEMENT, REPORT. CHRISTMAS EVE HUMILIATION SCENE PLANNED THE MIME TELLS REPORTERS. SCANDAL LOOMS.

New York, N.Y., December 2. S. Vireo, known popularly as the Child Pantomimist of Staten Island, will kneel in the snow on Christmas Eve before Serendipity, a well-known high-tone eatery and dispensary of chic "in" gifts for the sole purpose of "melting the heart and convincing the mind" of the posh outfit's owner, C. Zolt, who cashiered the mime-pantomimist after the greatest single scandal ever recorded in the East 60's. The outrage, which has reached the shores of Europe, was recently written up in the *Observer,* which gave the incident three columns in an article titled "Changing Weathervanes in the U.S.A."

British readers, who may not have known of Child-Mime Vireo, or of Serendipity, were given a fairly comprehensive résumé in the *Observer* as follows: Penniless and hungry, yet more than talented, Pantomimist Avante-Gard Vireo came one weary autumn day to appeal to Mr. Zolt to allow him at least to clean silverware in the sumptuous Serendipity

Kitchen with the lower classes. (Mr. Vireo has heatedly denied he said with "the other niggahs," but a witness says he said this, although S. Vireo's last-season intimacy with the well-known Trinidad wrestler Comstock Hart is still little less than a scandal.) Mr. Zolt at any rate somewhat misguidedly, in the opinion of his staff, gave consent, indeed *carte blanche.* Soon Mr. Vireo was out of the kitchen, flying hither and yon as a "better than wonderful" busboy, from a busboy he vaulted to waiter, and from a waiter to his claim to fame in the East 60's as a "nude, varnished, feather-boaed, eye-bandaged dummy" who rolled lettuce, tore skeins of wool and foamed at the mouth from a frail dais overlooking wary and often stomach-queasy patrons who complained his toenails needed cleaning and polishing (S. Vireo was always naked-footed during his seances at the restaurant).

Lightning struck in earnest when an elderly patron went mad and attacked the nude "dummy" Vireo. Pandemonium reigned for an hour. The noted heiress Madame Wenderholt was said to have hidden terror-struck in the men's powder room for five hours.

S. Vireo then resigned, and allowed police to interview him in his Staten Island professional "cave" where he teaches young men to be mimes and learn the "yellow hotfoot" (a Jamaican dance).

"I will go to Serendipity," Mr. Vireo told British reporters. "on Christmas Eve next, and kneel barefoot in the snow. I will not budge, gentlemen, until Mr. Zolt reinstates me as his *mime-extraordinaire,* and when that entrepreneur sees me kneeling in the snow, his cold heart will overflow, and he will take me, I reckon, to his bosom again . . . I only, after all, want to bring magic. There is not a harming-hair in my scalp. I want to bring joy to people, especially men, and I want to bring this to Serendipity, my home away from all my homes. This is my mission, my sole mission. I have no more to say, gentlemen of the media. Thank God, though, you are here to tell my sad oh-so-sad story. Tell it across the waves on Christmas Eve when my poor already chilblained feet will be frozen to the pavement in penitence. Pray God will touch Mr. Zolt and reinstate me . . . Godnight, gentlemen. A very fine holiday to you and yours . . ."

As a police spy and undercover agent (as well as a police shorthand expert and inspector of police archives), I find that Mr. Stephen Vireo, the noted Child Film Maker, formerly of the Blue Grass Region of Kentucky, was the director-producer of the following Illegal Motion Pictures, Old Rooster Studios, Lower Brooklyn, during the years 1971–1975:

AT THE FORK—(twenty-two minutes), A Story of Passion.

THE WOMAN WHO WENT—(forty-one minutes), A Study of A City Dilemma.

MY SON, MY SON, MY ONLY LOVE—(forty-eight minutes), Details incest in the Mountains.

HER CRUCIFIED NIPPLES, HER PAIN—A short film dealing in almost medical directness with madness.

EMMA HAZEL'S LATER REVENGE—The first real study of miscegenation leading to a razor fight, which is detailed in color.

THE BURN—(eighty-two minutes), A graphic study of a woman who could only know love when being branded.

UNCOVERED—Mr. Vireo's acclaimed film of a father's shame, the gambling disease, and the forensic approach to love.

IN THE PASTOR'S CABIN—(twenty-five minutes), An early study of the conflict between the cloth and the devil; tragic ending.

A WHITE WOMAN IN NEW YORK—One of Mr. Vireo's most acclaimed masterpieces; tells how a young white woman came to the Black Metropolis of New York City, her shame at being white, and her escape through the offices of a kindly mulatto transvestite.

LATENT—A thrilling study of a young heterosexual who married, had ten children, was happily married, and though puzzled mentally decided that he had always been heterosexual anyhow.

OFF WITH HIS SPOTS—Mr. Vireo's only nature study; studies the leopard in Africa.

RECTAL HEALTH IN THE LARGE METROPOLIS—Mr. Vireo's only non-art film, but technically brilliant; for medical students and doctors only. The part of the youth who plays the person afflicted with rectal detritus is the famous television star Rudolph VanSweringen. It made him a star. Write for rental fees to EMMA, Box 9, Grand Central.

AUNT SEREPTA—Shows the film maker as a baby of one week, nursing his Black Mammy. For private showing only. Rental fee, arranged.

S. Vireo's Minimal Demands for Props and Scenery for Any of His Proposed Film and/or Stage Ventures.[2]

[2] Originally proposed to Madame La Mama of the Voodoo Cafe (she rejected every demand except that of the pubic fringe of 8 world-famous French pugilists).

My Minimal Wants or Needs for My Next "Production":

12 hermaphrodite hyenas, young
400 clothes pins
1 Golden underage lion with pronounced testicles
1 hedgehog, unmated
300 Spanish shawls (Córdoba)
200 jars of early petunias, purple mostly
600 giant sunflowers just opened
40 corsets, all sizes, colors, not later than 1890
1 Ascending Balloon, decorated with scarlet hummingbirds
2 baboons either male or hermaphrodite
6,000 blue butterflies (ready to be released nightly)
800 Italian nightingales from Pisa
67 Ecuador parrots trained as ventriloquists
7 gladiators, not overdeveloped, and on the svelte side
1 native robin redbreast or turdus
12 bobwhites from the Atlantic shore
1 Peruvian mummy, in case
50 human skeletons, captains of infantry preferred
18 old-fashioned darkies (whiteheaded), with napkins over arms
½ ton of sequins, spangles and gold dust, mixed generously
8 stuffed white mice (pink eyes only)
200 ostrich plume fans
12 black bats (fox type)
89 middlesized elephant heads
1 cassowary (New Guinea only)
2 big ravens, trained
  or 14 young crows with clipped tongues, ready to talk
280 fresh Turkish towels
1 bag recently cut toenails of sprinters
1 bushel pubic fringe cut from the 8 leading living French pugilists
60 little dancing dogs in Persian skirts

Plus incense, gongs, tambourines, silk didies, piccolos, marimbas, mandolins, gaucho hats, artificial nipples, Argentine ropes and rawhides, brass knuckles, whiplash, etc.

FACE AT THE BOTTOM OF THE WORLD

BETSY ADAMS

To George Oppen

1
The blood engineer, the family:
faces in meadows   waiting

branch:
            the moon cut off
            Slice off ½ a tree:

                        is not a stump,
                        is not part
                        of the opaque surface.

The face at the bottom of the world
shines thru:

            its own sides   radiate,
            its own made crevices:

                        is not something exchanged,

is not a piece
of itself.

The eye brings to every small
collecting surface:

light:

drops of spectrum shift,
eyelashes remain intact:

brush borders,
flush with the system.

2

Gleams up a long tube, multiplies
the light of itself

folds:

must not fold upon itself.

The end of the face in a universe
does not seek for tube end:

the shine of a surface is pure,
is 100 percent,

only a remnant of what the face
is below the measured.

Mark this spot well, my child,
you will see it

in many equations,
in many correlations,

in many kinds of ways
saying you are:

And there is no one,

not the sun
not the moon

to block light from a tunnel:

Taking years of digging
perpendicular to the surface.

3
The face at the bottom
tiny splotch, suddenly radiates

light
in a spherical manner:

Blinding is:

it's as though sea studies
are necessary
in order to submerge.

Free faces, all in a row,
and the guy who sells the most

automatic discounting–
At most,
unreliable sources:

The code from the face,
the long tunnel of the face,
the lens of the face,
the bloody engineer

from a long l o n g focal point.

4
A correlation:

each red blood cell has a face
a face at the bottom
a face at the top
a janus face

My scope can see only one face
at a time:

opacity blocks
all light from the other side.

The members of my face
were defined long ago:

structure/function
the plus/the minus
assigned/you assign

I do,

friend: the face at the bottom
shines back:

Shatter (ing,ed)
1,000 fold

You do,

finally see correlations of yourself.

5
Thermoenergetics
and the reasons for death:

the branch
has no way to shoot off
no energy to give

one by one we resort
to the most insides of
the most insides.

I will,
and always there is
swamping of info:

a deluge
a loss of sequence.

An xs of a tree,
or of bone,
or of any coincentrically
laid substance:

the light comes off
in a regular, definable pattern,

numbers for each refraction
of light can be stated.

The face at the bottom
shines thru, the prime mover
in my life:

do not forget it

no matter how many ways,

learning to apply
circle within circle on top.

Note: xs = abbreviated form of cross-section

6
I brung my face for super exposure
super blow   up
all over the outside
(this guy, definitely, has
bucked teeth)

all over the outside
crummy tree stump

I brung all the best

up
up

windfall   swoop   apple
sinks into the grey dead

powders it   the stump
disintegrates

the apple

sinks   the teeth
at the bottom
always ready:

bite
bite   chomp!
(I need a metronome)

7
Who invited you here,
wind ripping off tree tops
and me
screwing around and around

sinking in snow

the tree stump
face sunk, bottom of it
sucks

me out

the world sinks
the trunk disintegrates
the teeth make:

    It is not a silver
    indelible map: etch perfect

    It is not the coincentric lines
    which are birth   ring
    upon ring   upon ring

    It is not: my mouth
    hungers
    for whatever the hell
    it is NOT

Face at the bottom of the world:
implanted
roots woven into the hide,
light finds its own tubes.

8
I erase,
one by one
the circle circumferences.

I smudge,
one by one
the edges so sharply defined
by years of growth. The edges

I pass off   onto you,
my friend:
parts of myself

and to you:
equally my enemy,
parts of myself.

The tree disappears,
the xs disappears.
Your view: personally
indefatigable

and amazing.

9
Loose edge   not force rip

edge   off   my hand:

thought
animal   hand
thought:

at 5 AM this morning
millions of cows, calves
sheep   pigs
will begin to be

slaughter:

my food:
my mouth:

my face floats at the bottom
of some swamp

of the anus
the food   the feces,
the poor dumb one that
gets stuck:

YOU MUST GROW A TREE,

it is not given to you

the tail
on the pig   he ran   swift
thought he was dog for the day
before

founder: pack:
the gnashing teeth of the pack.

I want to be up in the tree,
while I am down at its roots.

10
It is the trunk that supplies the
food   (via phloem)
water   (via xylem)

Face at the bottom of the world:

  Stump
  Cut off

  Facial roots:
  fed
      swamp water moccasins,
      light,
      and wild Ossabaw boar.

Face at the bottom of the world:

  Grow out, from certain,
  feelers, small branches:

  Stump: cut low on the trunk
           waist high on the man,
           is not the end of the man:

  the cambrium parallels
  the meristems implant

  The face: the focal polar point
  looking up   up   up
  out and out

Relays new environment:

The lost is lost
surroundings:
face at the bottom of the world:
surroundings:

Note: phloem = tissue in plants which carries food
xylem = tissue in plants which carries water
meristem = the generative tissue at top, bottom of plant
cambrium = the generative tissue of circumference of trees

TEN DRAWINGS

ALEKSEI REMIZOV

Introduced by Aleksis Rannit

Remizov, A Mannerist Drama

Aleksis Rannit

1

In the Renaissance an artist who was, for example, exclusively a painter could not possibly be recognized as a truly significant personality. Many artists of that period excelled in a variety of skills. Of them Leone Battista Alberti was probably the most outstanding. Besides being an architect who reached from Early to High Renaissance and even beyond, he was an accomplished art theorist, scientist, mathematician, calligrapher, painter, designer, poet, philosopher, playwright, athlete, canon of the Metropolitan Church of Florence, composer, and one of the foremost organists of his age. In recent centuries we do not have instances of such plentitude of talent bestowed on one person and we do not think it is important. We see no weakness in Ezra Pound because he could not draw, nor in H.D. that she could not sculpt. Nonetheless, the dream of *le violon d'Ingres* has persisted, and many writers have worked in other realms, especially as painters or graphic artists. The most obvious examples are Blake, Goethe, Lermontov, Edward Lear, Victor Hugo, Strindberg, Hopkins, Rossetti, Stanisław Wyspiański, Tagore, Valéry, Hesse, Cocteau, Lorca, Henry Miller, Wyndham Lewis, David Jones, E.E. Cummings, and Arno Vihalemm. Among these, aesthetic fullness—a convincing equality of talent in several fields—has been achieved only by a few like Lear, Hugo, Strindberg, Tagore, Wyspiański, Cocteau, Miller, and Vihalemm. The others are accepted masters in solely *one* sphere of art. Remizov belongs partly to these "others," but although resembling Blake, who was also greater as a writer, he is the purer artist of the two.

Aleksei Remizov was born in Moscow in 1877. He left Russia in 1921, never to return, and died poor and blind in Paris in 1957. One of the most original authors of modern times, he is still little known in the West. Banned in the Soviet Union, he is, however, admired in the Russian underground, especially by writers of the young generation. His work is variegated, but all of it is marked by his whimsical, mischievous personality. It includes novels in a neorealist manner, stylizations of old legends, the Apocrypha, the lives of the saints, and popular plays in which he displays neomannerist mastery of style and sound knowledge of baroque literature. Among the noted Russian writers of the past whom Remizov influenced are Zamiatin, Pilniak, Bulgakov, Leonov, and the later, ornamental Nabokov. Remizov proclaimed his own indebtedness to the works of Gogol (comic gift and surreal vision), Dostoevsky (religious ethics), and Leskov (*skaz*—peasant style of narration). He openly aimed at breaking the rigid forms of bookish grammar, reviving instead the intonations of living speech. However strikingly nonconformist and inspiringly "heretical" his writings are, especially with respect to his eccentric experimental language, his *image,* like that of Blake, is not complete without his graphic improvisations. This is particularly so because his contribution as an artist is, contrary to Blake's, stylistic rather than iconographic. And thus it is rewarding to read his metaphorical drawings and reflect upon their almost precious artistic fabric and their creator's poetic humor.

2

The exceptional quality of Remizov's unknown drawings in the Thomas P. Whitney Collection of Russian Art is demonstrated here by ten from the cycle entitled *Theater*. It consists of portraits of

Russian cultural personalities in exile, directly connected with the theater and theatrical in the sense of *commedia umana*. As a portraitist Remizov used two different styles in his nervous arabesque play of fancy, allowing an interchange between them. When the naturalistic image or figure passed into an ideographic symbol and his mimetic or representational preoccupation disappeared, the quality of Remizov's *picture writing* (as an abstract art) became dependent on the autonomous structural values of harmony, fluency, elegance, and interrelation of parts. This is especially true of the abstract sketch of Anna Pavlova or of the composition called "Mikhail Chekhov's Theater." In part that rhythmically spontaneous ornamentation is dominant also in the portraits of Boris F. Schletzer, the Russian and French man of letters (in French he signed his works as "de Schloezer"), of Nikita F. Baliev, the subtle humorous actor, shown in the drawing as an oriental personality from the cabaret theater Bat, of Fedor Chaliapine viewed in the role of Don Quixote, and of Mikhail Kashuk, Chaliapine's impresario and a manager of the Jewish theater Habimah. Kashuk's portrait is not pure embellishment *per se* but is still a flowing decoration.

The other drawings shown here are composed in contrast to visual immediacy, excessive exuberance, and notable attention to detail. They are accomplished by a slower, less vibrant hand and are much more the result of premeditation and interest in larger forms. From the lyrical (young Vladimir Nabokov, who at that time wrote under the pen name of Sirin) and melancholy (Alexandre Benois, the Franco-Russian painter-passéist, art critic, theater designer, and director), Remizov moves to a tectonically expressionistic mode (Ivan Khmara, actor of the Moscow Art Theater) and then to the very Remizovian chimerical grotesque (Konstantin Korovin, painter, theatrical artist, director, and costume designer). These four portraits with their heavy graphic linearity could be in fact realized as wood-cuts or linoleum-cuts. The decorative movement of the line is present but is no longer a dancing, undulating flame. In its Vallottonian or Masereelian nudity the line is poster-like, framed by broad and weighty planes of black. Here Remizov uses a schematic but vigorous pictorial technique—one which perhaps reveals the influence of primitive symbolism, folk art, and even Expressionism. What is missing, however, is the solidity and density of the archaic element so richly delineated in his literary work.

The portraits of Remizov, all of them spiced with mockery and histrionic ardor, are representations of images largely independent of nature, with the artist most interested in the ornamental singularity of the unreal or even abnormal and in transformation of his models into allusive and deformed masks. Mordant social comment is excluded; conscience expresses itself actually in the medium of caricature. There are also portrait scenes of witchcraft, which evoke the climate of the illusory meanderings of rococo and the genre of "magic drama," of *Los Caprichos* of Goya, or the fanciful intricacies of Hogarth's satirical genius (but without his bitter polemics). Remizov's own physiognomic *scherzi di fantasia* come, of course, from luxury and overabundance of *bizarrerie,* his excited pleasure in curiosities, and in fleeting and even irrational inventiveness. On examining his *Theater* it is difficult to draw a distinction between the formal values of the art of comedy and those of an experiential art of grace.

3

In Remizov, as in Gogol, we do not find much psychological insight; his characters are "flat" and resemble weird, strange marionettes. But contrary to Gogol's moral satire and also to Chekhov's twilight brooding, there is no sad humor in him; neither do we see in his work any Dostoevskian, very Russian, convulsions of the soul. Remizov's intention is *comic*—he is a nonsentimental Cyrano de Bergerac, staging a parody of oratory, his joke lying precisely in the contrast between the serious, or even sacred, nature of the subject and its conversion into the ludicrous. Like any true comedy, Remizov's relies for its effect on subtle irony, mythological imitation, and refined licentiousness.

Baudelaire has drawn for us a distinction between the "significative comic," which is dependent on references to the specific, and the "absolute comic" (the grotesque), which originates in fantasy, in art for art's sake. Remizov, who never had any formal art education, is amazingly enough an artist-aestheticist of the latter kind. The mannerist drama of his drawings is the art-conscious technical quest for virtuoso plurality and liberty of open forms. As such a craftsman he stands somewhere in the neighborhood of Cervantes and Molière, short of any cosmic pessimism or tragic declamation.

A tittering buffoon and sharp-witted jester, Remizov was convinced that he was a monkey. He identified his existence with that of monkeys, having, like them, amused the crowd without being understood. He invariably mirrored his entire self in those for whom life consisted in burlesque stylizations, in the very monkeyish *drôleries*. Having proclaimed himself supreme ruler of monkeys, he issued absurd calligraphic addresses and diplomas to his friends, making them honorary citizens of his imaginary imperium. Was Remizov familiar with the old Egyptian limestone groups of the Middle Kingdom showing odd monkeys in many parodied actions? I do not know. But he was one of them, a shamanic monkey indeed. Or did he play impractical jokes on us all?

Fedor Chaliapine (Shaliapin). India ink drawing, 2¾″ x 2¼″. (Thomas P. Whitney Collection) 1931.

Anna Pavlova. India ink drawing, 3½″ x 5¾″. (Thomas P. Whitney Collection) 1927.

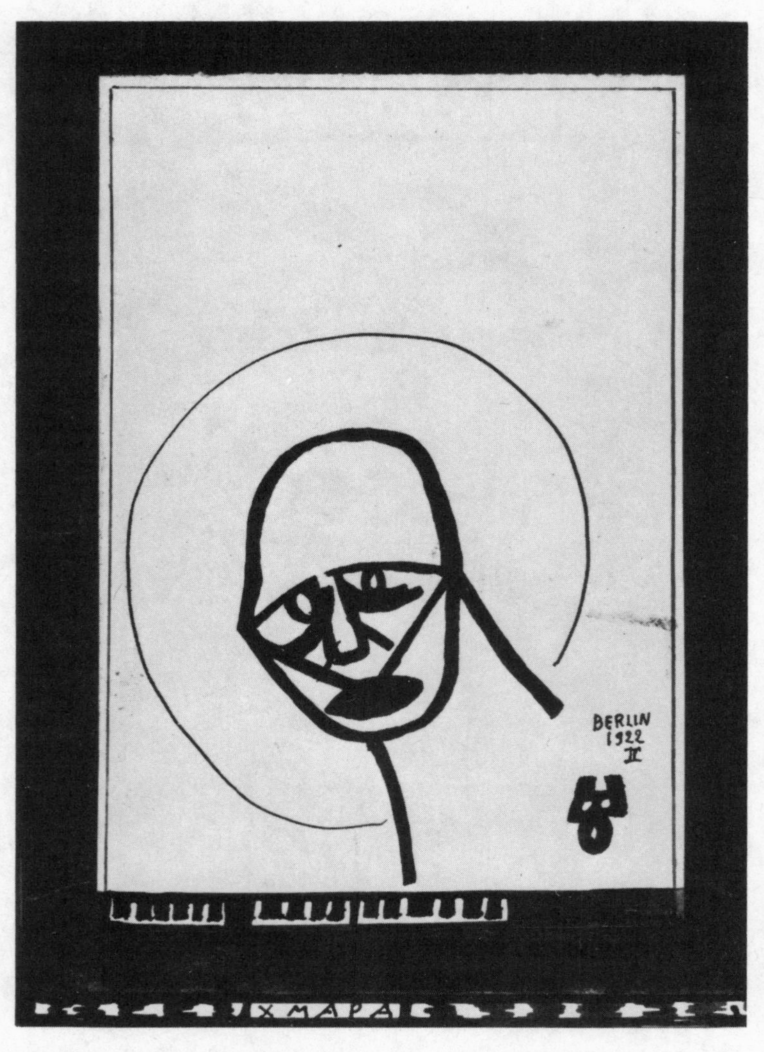

Ivan Khmara. India ink drawing, 4″ x 5½″. (Thomas P. Whitney Collection) 1922.

Mikhail Kashuk. India ink drawing, 2½" x 2½". (Thomas P. Whitney Collection) 1928.

Alexandre Benois. India ink drawing, 3¼″ x 6″. (Thomas P. Whitney Collection) 1929.

Mikhail Chekhov's Theater. India ink drawing, 6″ x 5″. (Thomas P. Whitney Collection) 1931.

Boris F. Schletzer. India ink drawing, 2½″ x 3½″. (Thomas P. Whitney Collection) n. d.

Konstantin Korovin. India ink drawing, 2¾″ x 2½″. (Thomas P Whitney Collection) 1926.

Vladimir Nabokov. India ink drawing, 3¼″ x 5″. (Thomas P. Whitney Collection) 1931.

Nikita F. Baliev. India ink drawing, 4″ x 8″. (Thomas P. Whitney Collection) 1929.

KLAUS VON STAUFFENBERG READS HIS PALM WHILE SHOOTING NIAGARA

PAUL WEST

Of the deaths a hero dies, these are the last. Born in Jettingen on November 15, 1907, I had a silky, aromatic, and gracious childhood deep in the bosom of an old Swabian family of devout Catholics. I lacked for nothing except some form of intolerance to goad me to a fine edge. At least that was how, swooning or wincing, I remembered my early days as I lay like a corpse with a high temperature in the hospital at Carthage. It was like having my childhood all over again, but in order to have a different adulthood after it, popped into a higher register or tempered for a chore not bargained for. I had still been born in Bavaria, yes, and I still was the third son of Graf Alfred Schenk von Stauffenberg, who descended from Hugo von Stophenberg, who showed up in a document dated August 21, 1262; but I was newer, a decade older, and animated by some force from outside.

All of a sudden I cared more about my father's having excelled at commonplace tasks around the family home than about his having supervised the abdication in 1918 of the king and queen of Württemberg to Bebenhausen. Once again I saw him papering rooms, tinkering with the maze of wires behind baseboards and plywood partitions, and even with chisel, mallet, and tenon saw repairing the furniture. Not that he was all sweetness and light; he could be genially sarcastic, even when he was weeding the paths of the estate at Lautlingen, pampering his roses, pruning the fruit trees, and in spite of the austerity of Alpine seasons managing to grow artichokes. He could be almost uncouth, especially when he and his brothers conversed, which they did through a ritual series of clipped growls incomprehensible to an outsider. He called this "signaling," and it shocked my mother when she first heard it, very much conscious that she had been Caroline Gräfin von Üxküll and was now trapped in some kind of bear garden. Yet her former name, Üxküll, had something of that same growling quality, between belch and a sotto voce command to some invisible wolfhound. Nor was I, in those days, better behaved, and even afterward I often neglected to shave or have my hair cut, and I cared even less about wearing a uniform of exquisite fit. Understandably, then, I never much cared how other people looked either, and it took me years to develop a knack for inspection; if my men seemed unkempt and untidy, they seemed natural enough to me, and I found no fault. I was sloppy, and I cared most of all about things of the mind.

That was my mother in me. Never quite in touch with court protocol or family mundanities, she lived in a world of Goethe and Shakespeare, quite often answering someone's questions as if she were speaking from within a play or a poem, and making an illustrious line (or even a speech!) do duty for her in the world of everyday. As lady-in-waiting to the queen, she remained diffident, always self-possessed in a starched sort of way, but mostly on edge, as if accustomed to a slightly different tribe of beings at a colossal distance from ours. "I will become an architect," I told her, and she nodded, as she did when I resolved to devote my life to the cello, and the trios began, with my brother Berthold on the piano and Alexander on the violin, the three of us making plaintively cumbersome sounds that veered between the lush and the strident. Eventually I gave up the cello, feeling that it was no use being a dabbler: if one wants to play such an instrument, one had better give one's life to it, and no second thoughts. But such thoughts came to me each month, and I moved on, becoming more proficient at reading than at music, not a cellist but a book-ist, although my Latin was always a little weak compared with my English, which was understood even in London and at the Royal Military College, Sandhurst. But I digress much as, there in Carthage, under the spell of that resonant name and tortured by multiple wounds that had every right to finish me there and then, I let my mind swarm all over me. Like some root fertilized with blood, I came laboriously back to life, perspiring, then shivering, which reminded me of our days in the old castle called Stauffenberg, now a ruin, in which we had a spacious suite of rooms on the second floor.

How cool the summers were in that massive, towered Renaissance hulk! How stark the winters, when, I think, our lips moved into conversation because they had twitched into a shiver. In the summers I learned how to scythe hay, and not only on level ground but also on the slopes. I had a favorite place, the "Felsentor," a prominent Alpine peak like a steeple amid the greenery of beech forests and the valleys below, in one of which the lazy old village nestled. Hiking for scores of miles, we fingered our region with our minds and senses, three brothers born into all kinds of responsibility, but most of all to the land and those who worked it. Why, we even spoke the Swabian dialect, and, after being away, began to speak it again as soon as we re-entered Swabia. Texture of earth: that's what interested me always, and the desert's texture came to me even as I lay blind, alternating twitch with rigid faint, like fine-ground broken glass in my eyes. I played pieces for cello in reverse, repeatedly fell into the summit of the Felsentor, and heard my father hammering at the plywood partition that walled me up in the old family castle never to be seen again.

Yet more frivolous dreams came too, and by no means because I was feeling better. No: there was an initial slab of time in which, at an almost total bodily halt, I did vertigo mental solos, an aviator without a plane. We, my brothers and I, were submitting to our theater craze all over again, not merely going nonstop to the old Royal (which had kept its name even after the Württemberg monarchy gave way to a republic), but also acting in plays, or bits of plays, in the drawing room at home. We lived, after all, in a palace that was a relic from a fabled era, and it seemed an ideal place for something theatrical. When we did act four of *Julius Caesar*, I played Lucius (a chance to play my cello as well) opposite Berthold's Caesar's Ghost and Alexander's Brutus. The overwrought Brutus asks Lucius to play something for him, but sees how sleepy the lad is and says, "I know young bloods look for a time of rest," to which I respond, now as then, "I have slept, my lord, already." Three lines later, I fall asleep! And I sleep all through the apparition of Caesar's Ghost. What should haunt me more, though, is the moment in the second act when Lucius admits the conspirators after Brutus says "Let 'em enter." I wasn't asleep *then*.

Years later, when I was in the Carthage hospital, hovering between the living and the dead, act one supplanted act four, and various garbled versions of lines from one and five washed everything else from my head:

O setting sun,
That thunders, lightens, opens graves, and roars
As doth the lion, thou dost sink tonight
In his red blood, most like this dreadful night . . .

Clank went the words in some gigantic metal tunnel in which the amplified sound of my pulse racing made a hectic counterpoint. I was dying, I knew. I was beyond pain, but some jumpy impetus, like frost at its most abstract, kept going through me, and something as trivial as my constant throat infections took its place in the full concert of bodily harm. Stauffenberg was hoarse again. His too light voice kept contradicting his vigorous, manly image. Cough, cough, my throat was always too narrow for something that lodged there like a bird in a gutter. I could never quite clear my voice, and after an hour's speaking (I was nothing if not talkative, and a loud laughter as well), I had to force every word into the outside world. Needless to say, every fever struck my vocal cords and my most irresponsible dream was of never needing to talk again.

Yet the schoolboy actor in me, this time in the school production of Schiller's *Wilhelm Tell*—which play the Nazis banned for silly, infected reasons banned—ranted out the part of Stauffacher. "No, there is a limit to a tyrant's might! When the oppressed can find no justice here below, when the burden becomes intolerable, then he will summon the courage to reach up to the heavens themselves and there grasp those eternal rights which are as unchangeable and indestructible as the stars in the sky . . . We must defend the highest virtues against all and every power."

Prophetic? Of course not, but I am amused to look back on the coincidence, which looks forward to a speech about stars by Heisenberg himself. An entire generation of German boys had parroted that speech, no doubt without thinking overmuch about what it meant and might come to mean. It was part of my heritage, no part of my fortune mysteriously told by the illustrious Schiller.

Most extraordinary of all, even as I felt the blood from my eyes pour over me again and two steel rods enter my ears in order to raise me to some kind of sitting position, I was in the middle of Christmas 1922, just after attaching holly and tinsel to the walls and windows of our drab little schoolroom. Silently the lights of the Christmas tree lit up. We read aloud the passage from the Epistle to the Corinthians 1:13: "and though I have all faith, so that I could remove mountains, and have not charity, I am nothing." Then we recited some poems of Hölderlin, joined hands, and sang with our teachers in a ring round the Christmas tree. It might have been a campfire in the Alps, into which we had slung our makeshift spears while ritually intoning lines of poetry or gibberish of our own invention. Life hummed with crackling joys, and our parents awaited us with gifts fresh from Ali Baba's cave.

2

Have I, I kept asking in my delirium (or hearing it asked on my behalf by some impossibly aloof reindeer at present in Carthage), *had a life?* Is there going to be any more? Or was that it, so poorly remembered? A wraith of a life, if even that.

There came no answer but the facts, as if I had been looking myself up, a ghost in the reference room. I read on, and on, and I soon began to believe that I had actually *been.* Two years after the twins Berthold and Alexander went to the Eberhard-Ludwig Gymnasium in the royal capital, Stuttgart, it was I who followed them, to learn Latin and read widely in poetry, philosophy, and classical history. It was indeed I of whom, at thirteen, and my brothers at fifteen, Caroline Gräfin von Stauffenberg, our mother, sent a photograph to the poet Rainer Maria Rilke, who wrote back saying we were "in many ways lads with a future." All lads have a future, but he was right beyond that commonplace, even if he was only being polite. I would be shot, and Berthold would be hanged only three weeks afterward, but in such very good company. It was as futuristic as that.

At seventeen, I moved into the circle of yet another poet, Stefan George, who had a profound influence on all three of us, catalyzing the lawyer in Berthold, the historian in Alexander, the assassin in me. In 1926 I became a military cadet after matriculating, and thus a part of the miniature army, one hundred thousand strong, permitted Germany by the humiliating Treaty of Versailles, and in particular the Seventeenth (Bamberg) Cavalry Regiment, in which, after first serving in the ranks and then attending the infantry school in Dresden and the cavalry school in Hannover, I was commissioned as a second lieutenant on January 1, 1930. After that, I went on another course, this time devoted to regimental close support with gun platoons. Strangely enough, I emerged as a peacemaker of sorts, and I felt much happier dealing with men than with things, which an architect would have had to do. Philosophy in action dealt with temperaments, not lumps of stone, and I felt this even more when promoted to full lieutenant on May 1, 1933. Then, on September 26th of the same year, I married Freiin Nina von Lerchenfeld in Bamberg's historic St. Jakob church. My life was filling in in a wholesome fashion; I had moved backward into the old Bavarian aristocracy and forward into the future, which included an advanced equitation course at Hannover, where I was obliged to ride four horses each day, two from school and two of my own. With my father-in-law, Baron von Lerchenfeld, who had been consul general in Shanghai, Warsaw, and Kovno, I bought a horse, Jagd, whom we chose as a foal at the stud farm and trained to meet the highest criteria for dressage.

Training Jagd from day to day was a delight, and the finest register of our movements together—all that bunched muscle flexing and tapping with butterfly precision—brought me to the point of ecstasy. It felt almost illicit as, with a snort and a sudden concentration of raw energy upon a single point, we did what should have been impossible, crossing the frontiers between the species. Coaxing her was a new rhetoric, and managing to draw from her such prodigies of discipline as the piaffer (in which the horse trots in place with a high action of the legs) was an almost saintly avocation. Jagd's strict impetus was one of the virtues of Creation, akin in my thinking to the poise with which certain pilots land or the accuracy with which certain archers hit the bull's-eye. When she moved or halted, I sensed intricate and heavenly design, a potential in the matrix of created things, a potential always there and awaiting a horse and a rider to tap it. Dressage was articulate rhythm, embroidery done with an instrument of brute force, and I became expert at it because it always had this metaphysical aspect. Indeed, in 1935 I came top in my class in the subject, and in so doing beat several members of the team which eventually won the 1936 Olympics.

But that was merely a triumph on the scoreboard, whereas the true magic of dressage had something in common with winning good from evil or, if not quite that, at least honing raw material into lustrous form. It was like owning a chunk of Creation's original masonry and being obliged to fashion out of it something that included strains of poetry, landscape, and fidgety trust. The horse's name meant "hunt," of course, but I consecrated her—as I realized after a year or two—to equine architecture: I was building, or designing, with heaves and checks, with lunges and retreats, with blood and muscle and bone. That horse was my Stonehenge, my Beethoven, my Rodin. In the privacy of my quarters, I would pretend I was the horse and, on all fours, attempt the most complex of the movements we did together. Ungainly and muscularly uncouth, I nonetheless began to understand what it was that Jagd had to do each time we went out to practice or to compete. I myself was not equal to such superfine tensions, and the spectacle of a tall cavalry officer doing the piaffer on the buffed brown parquet of his room, with high-stepping leg motions, was something no horse would relish. Never mind: he who rides must also be the ridden, or there is no merging, no symmetry. Jagd was momentum, I her in-the-saddle architect. And, sometimes, when I was at my best, I was a little bit *her* momentum, as when she was so precariously perched that the merest part of her own force would have been too much, and I would move her back or forward with just a finger's weight, and we executed the maneuver perfectly, which a floating feather would have wrecked. Exaggeration? Of course, but it shows the extent to which dressage became my catechism. There was always a perfection beyond the one achieved, and I regretted the time we had to spend with guns and tanks, or even on preparing for the English interpretership examinations.

Not that I despised the concept of many-sidedness. I was always going to concerts and lectures, dabbling with my cello, devouring art, literature, politics, history, philosophy. I needed all of it, convinced that the human brain can be stuffed and stuffed. There is no imaginable surfeit, there is only the dismal prospect (in my own case, now retrospect) of never having enough time to come near the outskirts of a maximum. In my immodest way, I soon realized that intellectually I was as different from my fellow officers as Jagd from me. Therefore they needed me even more, to settle disputes, to point out what was idiotic and what was wise, to separate what was scurvy from what was honorable. Was I actually some sort of moral locum tenens to my contemporaries in the Bamberg cavalry? I suspect so. I no doubt showed off. Articulate people do. I regaled them all with the sound of my voice. I was the historian of dressage: I told them all they needed to know, and much of what they didn't. Yet there were certain men I kept aloof from, in spite of their repeated overtures; something either violent or underhand kept me from them, even though, to their utter bewilderment, I camouflaged aversion with my legendary infectious, extroverted laugh. I was a jolly fellow they just could not get to know, and so they decided there was nothing more to me than laugh, ride, and drill. All the same, I could see some of them, gaping bemused as the edge of my intellectuality showed in talk with someone else, in a swift allusion to Propertius or Livy, to Leibnitz or Shakespeare, and it became clear that I was suppressing a self they would never know, not even at second hand. Not that my fellow cavalrymen understood much of what I said when I became especially allusive, but they took it all in good part as, I suppose, the involuntary electrostatic effect of a garrulous mind. In fact, within my most private self, I held nonstop conversations about the most rarefied matters, from the punctuation of poetry to the responsibility of an aristocrat. I was no intellectual dynamo, I who, in spite of private tutors at Lautlingen, when the delicate health of my early childhood had kept me from school, scored only the following grades as "external candidate" for the matriculation exam: Good in French, history, and mathematics, but only Satisfactory in the other subjects, and (shame, shame!) merely Adequate in Latin. But, I confess, I found the presence of my mind in my head increasingly exhilarating.

Very well, then, I was a popular pariah, an earthy aristocrat, a conservative addict of the new. Commanding my mortar platoon in training, I was just as competent as I had been in Latin, say, but I am aware that I occasionally let rip with sarcasm or, if not that, an irony well short of genial. If you have too much mental energy, you cannot have only one career, or only one obsession. I knew this, and then I began to worry about whether or not one can have multiple obsessions, and, if so, what kind of person one became—polymath or dilettante, as if to say, Everything done with shallow brio. Not I, let us hope. I was my own political party, my own disputant extraordinary; after all, as a soldier under the Weimar constitution, I had no vote. I was certainly not among those, however, who addressed lax elegies to the Kaiser on his abdication to Doorn, or who opposed the removal of the Hannover riding school to Krampnitz, near Berlin, so that an airfield might take its place. As for those of my fellow aristocrats who maintained that the king of Bavaria was the only leader to whom we owed allegiance, I scoffed at them and, when on leave among my relatives in Franconia, I would wear my uniform simply to show them where I stood. Nor, *echt* conservative that I was, did I ever join in the fun poked at the black, red, and gold flag of the Weimar republic; I never called it "black-red mustard."

No: *res publica,* as even my "Adequate" Latin told me, meant "the public thing," the entity that corresponded publicly to all the swarming thoughts within. It was our public face, and, by God, I said we should not let it be seen to be sneering, giggling, or gnashing its teeth. It was all we had with which to construct something even better. Somewhere along the line, you have to take a wild or a drab or an undernourished horse and groom him into dressage; without the horse, you do the antics in mid-air or, in an abortive dead-end fit on the floor, in the sealed privacy of your room.

So, when someone suggested that I run the local youth movement, I refused, saying, "I am not interested in ideas, only in human beings. The 'idea' of the youth movement has no appeal for me. Sorry." It would have been more honest to say that a horse was not a concept and that I did not perform gymnastics, in public or in private, with ideas in grease paint. Several of my contemporaries went on to become priests, which is to say they found their true vocation early, whereas I had a vocation whose effect would have to be special, so final, that I had to obey various preliminary "callings" in order to come close to it at all.

3

Three episodes, two from 1933, the year of my marriage, the other from 1934, remind me who I was, and what. The first happens to be a legend, first aired by Peter Sauerbruch, son of the famous surgeon, and can be dismissed as mere gossip from the officers' mess. It says that, on January 30th, I put myself at the head of a procession to hail the birth of the Nazi regime. I did nothing of the kind; indeed, as an officer I was not permitted to involve myself in Party demonstrations, whether by torchlight or not. The fact is that, on January 31st, the Fifth Squadron of our own Seventeenth Bamberg Cavalry was riding back to barracks from maneuvers, under the command of a certain egregious extrovert named Hasso von Manteuffel, a captain. On passing the Town Hall, where Nazi zealots had raised the swastika flag, Manteuffel gave the order to ride to attention—stiff-backed and taut-lipped in the crisp swill of January air, with the horses gasping and coughing as their perspiration cooled—in the mistaken belief that the swastika had been elevated to the status of the national emblem. In fact the swastika did not become "legal" until 1935.

Later, Manteuffel received what he himself called a "severe downright reprimand" from the regimental commander, Freiherr von Perfall, in front of the assembled officers, for this bit of misplaced punctilio. One does not give commands, even the command to ride to attention, on the strength of rumor or hearsay. Captain von Manteuffel had failed to check his sources, as historians say. Either way, as Perfall told him, he should have done nothing: "This is, after all, a revolution," he said forcefully, "and we can have nothing to do with it."

With the merest nod of self-rebuke, Manteuffel took his punishment, needing perhaps only a course in elementary German grammar to enable him to conduct a squadron of horses through a lively town.

On the previous day there had indeed been a torchlight parade through Bamberg, all the way from the outskirts to the Maxplatz. When it reached Chain Bridge, catcalls and whistles were directed at it from below, where those hostile to the regime had gathered. In the town square, the usual claptrap rhetoric poisoned the night air when a member of the town council, Zahneisen by name, lauded the Party's thirteen-year growth, vowed that S'gruber would remain Reich Chancellor for as long as he wished, and that the Party would persist in its ruthless struggle for absolute power. They clinched their Roman jamboree with a triple Heil and an untidy rendering of the national anthem. There was no officer at the head of this carefully manufactured rabble. Nor should there have been. Defendant Stauffenberg acquits himself herewith. My own squadron was the *First*, not the Fifth, in any case.

As for Manteuffel, however, some of my fellow junior officers sympathized with him, as indeed with any premature obeisance to the Nazi seizure of power from the properly constituted authorities. They foresaw the restitution of our national rights (not necessarily a bad thing for a nation for too long restricted to gliders and an army of chocolate soldiers), and especially a defense force equipped (as the Reichswehr certainly never had been) with modern weapons. The soldierly virtues would come again into their own, and a country long divided against itself would begin to heal. No one spoke much then, or even thought, about territorial expansion, although such adventures must have been implicit in the fervor with which we all, myself included, looked to National Socialism. The first act of the drama was clear: renew national sovereignty. The second act might be martial, or it might not.

What concerns me, however, is the way in which Hasso von Manteuffel vanished into the porousness of history while his blunder became my own. It has always been my habit to look at things critically, and, even when I agree with a certain point of view, to enact as forcefully as possible the opposite point of view in the privacy of my own mind, or in conversation with a few selected intimates. I have since then realized how easily one can thus gain a reputation for vacillating, for playing both ends against the middle. It is the fate of the balanced mind, I suppose, of the man who has too active a mind ever to become the mouthpiece for a single doctrine. "For the sake of argument," was how I began so many sentences. I even queried Nazi changes in the Wehrmacht uniform. The Nazi eagle-above-swastika replaced the familiar cockade, and the very sight of the Reich's warflag colors—black, white, and red, wreathed in oak leaf—was enough to make me exclaim, "Even worse things might follow this measure. We should consider it most seriously." On the one hand, Nazism promised to rid us of the crust which bourgeois habits had become, but, on the other, my own weird and patchwork idealism, as lofty as it was discursive, held me back. I certainly did not want to become a servant, a menial, a gullible dog's-body, in any proletarian surge, and I was anxious to protect the interests of the nobility even under a trade-union regime. What was urgent, however, was that Germany move forward, acquire some impetus (from whatever source), and then refine its polity later on. Judged by too many to be a devout National Socialist, I was always much more complicated than that. Stauffenberg Castle near Hechingen dates back to 1262. I am of the old Swabian nobility. My father was a high official at the court of Württemberg and later became marshal of the court to King Wilhelm II of Württemberg. My mother, God bless her for poetry, was no less than the great-granddaughter of Gneisenau. When you have Prussian field marshals behind you, you do not grovel, you do not take orders from a paperhanger.

The question, then, is why I did. Some things have misted over: perhaps the Bamberg incident took place in March, after the swastika had been illegally decreed the national emblem. One sometimes is not even sure about how many fingers are on one's hand. At any rate, let it be said at once, I went along with the new regime. Oh yes, I prated of some common good we all aspired to; I even admired the energy and drive of the new nationalism and went so far as to agree that those who did not work should not eat, that blood and soil were sacred, that some forms of life were not necessarily to be cherished. My brothers and I agreed that Jews were different from "us," and should be guided into a separate existence, although without extremes of cruelty. When I look back, I am amazed by how many ill-assorted workers and mercenaries, Catholics and nationalists, nobles and burgers, xenophobic maniacs and opportunistic sadists, honorable military men and shameless militarists came together under the crude, corrugated-iron roof of master-racism and *Lebensraum*. It was a fit of national poeticism gone cancerous. It was surely something much more grievous than what Berthold said in 1944, claiming that "The basic ideas of National Socialism were almost all turned into their opposites by the way the regime implemented them." *That,* from a lawyer. Surely there was something wrong not merely with the implementation, but with the ideas themselves. We knew better, but we had been in the doldrums too long, and vigor was manna.

The second episode, also from 1933, might explain in part my eccentric behavior in those heady days. I had done a dandy's quickstep into the army, yes; but I had also moved into a much more pensive dimension as well, and in fact, on December 4th, with my two brothers and eight friends, I was at the deathbed of Stefan George, in Minusio near Locarno. The Nazis had claimed him as an ideologue, much to his perplexity and embarrassment, so as his sixty-fifth birthday approached he decided to get out of the way. So as to be unavailable on July 12th, he left Bingen on the 8th and went initially to Berlin. From there he traveled to Wasserburg on Lake Constance, next to Heiden im Appenzel, and then to Minusio, his habitual winter resort, in September. How many times, at café tables, with our strong coffee gone tepid in the wind that brings color to the cheeks and mysteriously fans the mind's glowing coal, had we not seen the blue tinge of his facial skin? We had turned to him as if he were a sundial. His head was lordly, like an exquisite massif. His drab skin had no wrinkles, taut as it seemed. His face had many angles of bone. His shock of hair, brushed back, was black rather than gray. His hands were pale, those of a gesturing invalid at odds with the resonant baritone of his voice. His long double-breasted frock coat had two clasps at the top, open to reveal a cravat of black velvet that overflowed the collar. On a ribbon that tethered a monocle or a watch, he wore a discreet gold toggle, and his elastic-sided shoes looked tight enough to have been sprayed on. He always seemed unapologetic for knowing almost everything. Youthful supermen, we spoke austerely with him about the antagonism of mind to soul and the need for a national leader to focus on. Far from the Nazis in his pajamas of indeterminate bluish hue, he was just as far from us, who had come to pay him tribute, receive whatever blessing he had. His breath had a flavor of burnt paper. His eyes were blank as fingernails, with dead-iris moons. And his hands hardly moved at all, seeming when they did to be stirred this way and that by some invisible current.

Had it not been for that lost leader, that energumen of the lyrical mind, would we have been such easy meat for the paperhanger, whom I here call S'gruber? I doubt it. The death of Stefan George in December 1933, six months after I had been promoted to full lieutenant, removed not only a mentor and an idol, but also (I find it hard to phrase this exactly) a point to steer by: a lodestar, a Canopus, a tropic, a pole. No longer would he give us his cautionary look, yawn at the sheep-gray sky, then read us half a dozen poems in which a bud erupted, a son came home, ripe fruit thudded to earth, almond trees came at once into blossom, rigid air collapsed around a house. A well called sorrow. Two dusky moths. A full moon. Grapes.

"Snoring in the bowels of a mountain," George said, "the absent leader bides his time." And then he came, improving garbage heaps into cesspools, providing psychopaths with a new bauble called the law. But all that was later, when our eyes began to work again. With George gone, a certain poetic streak in us became homeless. Was that it? Even though his poetry lived on? A genius died, and a charlatan usurped the role of god. I would better have reread the classics, studied music more intensively, ridden a wider variety of horses, or gone to New York to look at skyscrapers, than to have sucked at the teat of Nazism. I was not so much duped as I was a sleepwalker. Deep down I wanted a king, not a Führer, a Franconian and Swabian court, not a star chamber of gangsters. Easy to say; impossible to know at the time.

In fact, the poet had designated Berthold his heir while Goebbels, as wetnurse to the new Germany, had made slavish use of George's name in propaganda stunts. So it was not improper of us, in accordance with the Tessin custom, to stand watch, with our friends, day and night round the deathbed of the man who had invented our minds and made them work like waterfalls. I myself drew up the roster for our two-day watch. He had called us an elite, and now we paid elitist homage.

Only a year later, well aware that I was in for a guttersnipe orgy of invective and filth, I was detailed with a friend to represent the regiment at a Nazi demonstration in Bamberg. It was Party Day, and the first speaker was Reichsleiter Schemm, followed by the Nuremberg Gauleiter, Julius Streicher who, in front of several hundred undeveloped minds from the German Girl League, inveighed against the Jews in such revoltingly scatological language that my brother officer and I got up and walked out down the center aisle. Here was a boil we would have to lance. I regret only that we took so long to pick up the scalpel. In effect, the two-day watch at the deathbed of the poet we adored became one of five years, and our timebombs were fused with lovely metaphors drenched in guilt. Yet, if we were slow, so too were gullible Oswald Spengler and Karl Barth, two minds with but a single gape.

As a leisurely observer in the countryside around Lautlingen, I had many times seen and wondered at the tiny mechanisms at work when a squirrel gave itself a high-speed shoulder scratch or, while looking ahead, rippled the bush of its tail. That was what, in our dainty uniforms, we kept on doing for years, even while the signs of trouble multiplied. The SA saw itself as the Praetorian Guard of the new society, yet all we did (we being the army) was to try to distract it from its pogroms by engaging it in night maneuvers and to hamper it by denying it access to the secret caches of illicit weapons on estates all over the country (I myself made trucks available for the removal to even safer places of the caches in the Bamberg area). A rival army grew alongside us. The army protested with increasing vehemence until S'gruber wiped out its leaders all in a matter of a few hours. We should have learned from that. We were all expendable, as I said to my squadron commander, Lieutenant Colonel Hans Walzer.

"One can only remove such a regime by force from above," I remember telling him, although without the faintest intuition of the part I would eventually play in such an act. "The man has destroyed democracy with democratic methods."

"Once upon a time," Walzer was musing, "we thought he would be just the man to put an end to party political wrangling. Look at us now!"

"Yes," I said, rather bitterly. "Just look out there," as I waved vaguely at the countryside, with that image of the squirrels uppermost in mind. "The Treaty of Versailles gave him a licence to practice. And to preach, of course."

Walzer stared forlornly through the glass at the gathering greens of summer, with nothing to say, either before or after I vented my feelings in an unco-ordinated, gaudy outburst that went something like this: "The squirrels seem to manage it. No parties. No books. No rallies. No communists. No flags. No swastikas. No Streicher. The squirrels have no Jews."

4

Of the deaths a hero dies, these are the last. "Kill him," I said in July 1942, meaning the Führer, the one I call S'gruber. So simple a proposal created a new simplicity in the faces around me. Everyone was trying to think up some adjustment, some stratagem, and here I was delivering my old absolute remedy. It was easier said than done, of course, yet for peculiar reasons it seemed easier to me than to many others. Was it because, deep down, I always knew that it would be my own hand that armed and placed the bomb?

From early adolescence I had felt I was cut out for something extraordinary: not in poetry, music, or architecture, though each was a passion with me, but this—a feat of arms, never mind how underhand, never mind how inconspicuous. It connected itself to the pith of history, a peripheral event that affected everything my own century did or thought, even at the end of 1942 when the military situation had become hopeless. When, like a fool, I was visiting the spineless Manstein at Taganrog on the Sea of Azov, I had said something about being eager to get back to the front. Since 1940, although much of the time in Russian territory, I had been attached to the Organization Section of the General Staff. There were too few of us, and of these too many were out of touch with both military and civilian affairs. Besides, I was weary of headquarters prattle, of the flinty lap of Mother Russia, of the *débâcle* at Stalingrad. Perhaps I wanted warmth. If so, Tunisia was just the place; but nothing distracted me from my gathering obsession, and when someone asked me what on earth we could do about S'gruber's dreadful and disruptive way of running the war, I said once again the honorable, simple thing: "Kill him!"

Dreaming or musing thus, I left Munich early in February 1943, transferred to the Afrika Korps, where I was to be staff officer (Operations) of the Tenth Panzer Division. My predecessor, Colonel Wilhelm Bürklin, had been badly wounded after driving over a mine on February 4th, and Lieutenant General Wolfgang Fischer, who had been with him, had been killed. So it was very much a case of moving into a dead man's desert boots. Praise be, I was never superstitious, although, while I went about my duties in a light staff car, I had constantly to keep at bay lugubrious thoughts about the war, already lost on both the Eastern and Western fronts and far from won there in the desert. I tried to keep an open mind.

This was no Greece, where I had once taken a few hours off and, with a friend, driven to the coast for a swim. We found a soft-sanded cove full of our own soldiers, Alpine troops who had been in Norway. For a while I stood there on the headland above them, looking at their bronzed nudity as they swam and threw a ball about (they like some parody of Stefan George's Ancient Greece). They looked back and up, some self-consciously, some with a kind of breathless insolence. Then I gave them a wave and left them to their sport. My friend and I found another spot to swim from, private and calm.

This was no place, either, in which I could once more listen enraptured to a Cossack choir, or savor the honor as Russian troops danced for me in front of their campfires. Nor was it one of those mild saunters I had become accustomed to, as guide to foreign military missions. I had just missed the battle for Dunkirk, but I wasn't going to miss this one. This was work, and danger, and what I was born to. The uniform was different too: no more of the colored piping which, contrary to ignorant supposition, does not spoil one's camouflage, whereas against a terrain of wholly uniform color—such as the desert—it fails to blend. As a Panzer officer, however, I could wear, though I didn't bother to, the corps emblem: a death's head made of aluminum; I would have preferred the gold Burmese dragon of General Wavell's "Chindit" Division, or the dislocated rhinoceros of HQ East African Expeditionary Force, to this cut-out of a petulant monkey canted to the right. But the beret, yes, that was quite acceptable, and the lightweight lace shoes would come in, even though both were intended for men in tanks, in which I would not be. However dressed, Lieutenant Colonel Stauffenberg was going to war again, with coiled braid, one star, and on my lapel patches the regimental number where the Death's Head should have been. I glowed with prowess and heat.

5

It was a new world: hot, silent, dusty, tame; and military action seemed a loutish and unforgivable temper tantrum in the hinterland of a sublime playground. Surely, I thought, this is no place to be blowing one another to bits. It is a place to come and think, to be Job or St. Anthony, from which to view the stars while flat on your back, to study the molden vignettes in mirages. Tanks moved across the desert like some disintegrated conveyor belt still moving, although its parts had lost contact with one another. The belt had a rhythm of its own. There was debris everywhere, stunted and uncannily chaste as if no hand had worked this field gun with its torn barrel or that buckled motorcycle with its khaki sidecar ripped in half. I learned a new music, which was the solid churn of the Panzer, crunching sand with its perpetual-motion iron treads. In Russia, whose summers I forgot, snow had muffled everything, but here sound came into its own, and the silence over the dunes was wholly unlike that over the snow. The silence blazed vacant and upward into the never-ending blue, whereas in Russia the sound seemed always unable to lose itself and hugged you as you moved about. In the desert, a heard thing moved away from you as soon as heard, having too much room to move about in. In Russia, sound was a cozy fetish; in the desert a fluid stranger. I was glad to be in a place where the sun had not vanished into some abyss above us, but plastered us nonstop, made metal impossible to touch, made perspiration blind you by day and sudden chills wake you at night. The sturdiest of communication planes, the Fiesler "Storch," became a familiar sight, always flying low, an aircraft a plumber might have thought up, not so much ungainly as littered with afterthoughts, so much so that it might have doubled as a tractor or a launch-pier for a rocket. I saw men sleeping alongside a tank's treads and one man trimming another's hair with a safety razor while both stood on a blanket as if to protect the sand. Trousers aired on the barrels of tanks' 75-millimeter guns. Rubber-kneed soldiers floundered upward in sand dunes or crouched for cover alongside ammunition boxes stacked behind a wall. I took a stand-up bath with my feet in an enamel basin, accomplishing my entire ablutions with two or three liters. Incongruous juxtapositions found a permanent home in my brain, from naked soldiers gurgling at a well, with clumps of untidy thornbush at their feet, to a dump for tires that looked like leftovers from some giant's game, from wounded tourniqueted soldiers huddled in a corner of a roofless house, with a black wooden cross behind them against the wall, to Italian tanks padded with sandbags to compensate for their inferior armor. We used everything we found in this zone of the imported; nothing we needed grew there of its own accord, and one had an acute sense of being merely a figure against an overpowering ground. Interlopers, intruders, but, more than either, arbitrary aliens whose own customs became stranger day by day, almost as if there were no appropriate region to return to. One did not belong in the desert, but through some weird reversal of the converse one did not belong anywhere else either. One felt a denatured human, newly made into a pariah in the middle of nowhere according to far-fetched rules. A salute in the desert was a vain wave at the sun. A pair of heels clicked was the shuffle of a lizard against the sand. A command was a long-level horizontal echo that went out and out, ranging over the impacted flatness and ending only God knew where. Words themselves were the meagerest signs in that enveloping fug. One felt very much on the surface of a *planet,* one of whose wastelands we were ploughing up to no visible end.

All the same, it took me only a few days to learn the ropes, adjust to the furious alternation of lull and combat. I saw how the 18-88 flak gun, used as an antitank weapon, had too high a silhouette and so had to be dug well in. The funnel-shaped clouds of smoke from burning tanks hung in the sky from day to day, creating unusually co-ordinated patterns of wedge and cone. Spatted and greenhouse-canopied Stuka divebombers took off from the roughest runways I had ever seen, pitted with scrub and shrapnel-like stones, but they always lurched into the air at the very last like birds of prey with broken wings. I took soup in the open at a makeshift table, with the hottest of spoons. I became accustomed to the aroma of musk, which made men smell like laundry, but I never got accustomed to the way in which one's underclothing went from soaked to stiff, from stiff to bonily unabsorbent and, when finally removed, made a faint tearing sound like adhesive bandage.

Far from the snow-wrapped atrocities in Russia and the lush greens of the Bamberg countryside, after a week I was an old hand, an old sweat, but after a month even more out-of-my-element than when I began. In the desert, I found, what you learn has no lasting power. The heat abolishes all improvised wisdoms. Desert warfare one can learn about, especially on the spot; but something . . . subtractive . . . in the atmosphere denudes you daily of what you think you have acquired. No doubt the famous Colonel Lawrence had written about this, in a book I never read. I know only that in the desert you are continually present at the hypothesis of your own absence, and your actually being there makes hardly the slightest difference. After two months, I was (I flatter myself) more than competent as an operations staff officer, but my sense of self had dwindled steadily from the end of the first week, and each day, when I was not intent upon some problem with a map and a wadi, a stalled tank and the new exigencies of tank warfare in hilly country, I sensed bits of me missing, as if a small cube of me that was there yesterday had fallen away. Dilapidation of the soul, I called it, but it was nothing compared to the dilapidation of the American First Armored Division when Tenth and Twenty-first Panzers, converging from two directions, enveloped it and, by February 17th, virtually wiped it out. Next thing, Tenth Panzer went off on a wild-goose chase to Fondouk, northeast of Kasserine; the British had already withdrawn. Then, with seemingly irrepressible gaiety, we were buying eggs from the Arabs. Thinking large, Rommel overwhelmed his more plodding fellow commanders, and his grand slam—Twenty-first Panzer, plus the Afrika Corps Assault Group, plus Tenth Panzer all ramming through Tebessa to the north—never took place. It might have made the Allies retreat right into Algeria. As things turned out, Tenth Panzer joined up with the Afrika Corps at Kasserine on the 20th.

Flying over the Pass, I marveled at the ripples of some gigantic geographic shrug that had heaved up the land for hundreds of miles. The way through, if such a term is appropriate, was rugged and steep. We failed to secure the heights on the 19th, but on the 20th my own Tenth Panzers broke through, pounded up the miserable road, destroyed the American defense as well as a British battle group en route to Kasserine, and ended the day nose-to-nose with the British Armored Brigade ten miles south of our objective. With Afrika Corps protecting our flank, Tenth Panzer then pushed back the British to within three miles of Thala, at which point exhaustion claimed us. The weather improved and Rommel, sensible of the renewed threat from the air, moved us back behind a screen of booby traps and demolitions. Compared to the Desert Air Forces and the U.S. Air Force flying from Tunisia, the Luftwaffe was in total eclipse, as was, for a while, Tenth Panzer. Short of tanks, we did battle once again, at El Guettar, where after an opening foray of stupendous momentum that carried us through to the American artillery lines, we paused to regroup and repair. That evening, Tenth Panzer set off again only to be just about annihilated by high explosive shells. Those tanks that could still move went to the rear. After that, with Twenty-first Panzer, we played cat and mouse with General Patton's resurgent Second Corps. On April 6th, the Eighth Army launched an all-out assault, and Fatnassa fell in one night to mountain-trained Indian troops. The entire front went up in flames. The Italians surrendered while Germans fought on, and our own higher command began to quarrel among themselves, blaming the Italians. Air attacks poured upon us from all points of the compass, strafing everything in sight, so much so that the ground troops could not move. There was nothing to do but retreat northward by night, and I found myself moving toward Gafsa with all the tattered panoply of modern strategy: map-cases, folding tables, dividers, protractors, files in steel boxes, and of course my own battered shaving things. In crumpled American trousers and an Afrika Korps shirt, hastily wiping mud and glass splinters off my maps, I must have been an unimpressive figure in the divisional command post (a caravan) in the olive grove west of Sidi Mansour. Was this the free-reined intellectual who, with his commander, Major General Freiherr von Broich, talked until midnight of literature, philosophy, and politics? I saw that question in the eyes of a young officer who reported to me on April 6th, right in the teeth of the combined British-American attack of the same day. In fact we were under artillery fire and, as soon as he entered the caravan, I stood and pointed out to him two foxholes not far from the window.

"If that starts up again," I told him, with a bland jollity I didn't quite feel, "you take the right one, and I'll take the other." I could hardly give him my best attention, trying to explain to commanders under fire that they could neither be reinforced nor retreat. We had no reserves, and we would have to hold the line until sunset if the Italians in the south were not to be swallowed up from behind.

"Yes, yes," I told my callers, "I too have been face down in the mud. I can hear infantry fire even as I talk to you. I'm sorry, but there is nothing we can do."

All the same, the dark side of desert warfare hovered just beyond the fringe of my mind's eye: soldiers actually lost in a sandstorm en route from a tent to the latrine, as if in echo of what had happened on polar expeditions; games of football, played by either side, ludicrously left uninterrupted by an ethic that respected the leather ball more than life itself; the eerie way in which, on the sand, we seemed to be using the principles of naval warfare, with no towns or cities to get in our behemoth way; the terrible sights to be found inside the inadequately armored British tanks; the nauseous and toxic stench of flies burning after being collected in millions by soldiers in special clothing; the charred driftwood littered about, which was in fact a pattern or trail of soldiers burned alive and then incinerated further by the sun for weeks, months, a year even. All this droned, hummed, rat-tatted in my head, especially when I had had too little sleep, and not even the belly laugh memory of Rommel's fake tanks, made of timber and painted canvas, lined up on the dock, or the full-dress dinner party the British obliviously staged when he entered Tobruk could cheer me up. I was tired of the constant search for an open flank to go round, whose erotic sound reminded me of privileges I dare not remember lest I misread a name on a map or issue the wrong orders to some poor devil with his head down behind a dune already thick with lead.

So it was something of a relief to chat with this newly arrived subaltern and, in a more or less teasing vein, to compare his previous experience—as a railroad transport officer—with where he found himself now.

"What do you think," I asked him with a smile, "is the point of your coming here to Tunis, *just now?* If any!"

His answer was the epitome of unamused candor. "I suppose, to get myself taken prisoner."

I laughed agreement. "That's it. We shall be lucky. That will be the end of the war for us." Then I sent him on his way, having once again insisted, in my not quite military gregarious way, on meeting everyone, whatever his rank. I have never agreed with the clinical view which says, if you have to order men to their deaths, it's better not to know them. I knew almost all of mine by name, which made me a sort of walking hotel register. The reason, perhaps, was that from the outset my Tunisian appointment had been an almost family affair. I remembered lunching at Kempinski's in Berlin, early in February, with my wife and Frau Beate Bremme (an old friend from Wuppertal) and my immediate predecessor's predecessor in Tunisia: Colonel Bürker, whom Colonel Bürklin had replaced, but only for a short time before being wounded. The lunch was effectively a handover from Bürker to myself. During the meal, they broadcast the army communiqué about the catastrophic events at Stalingrad, and both Bürker and I, with our wives gaping at us in uncritical astonishment, vented our feelings rather loudly, so much so that a waiter came over and (cheek!) demanded that we lower our voices. In fact we went on as before, and at greater volume. I have always been vocal, I suppose, having already cried out, some time earlier, "Is there no one at the Führer's headquarters capable of taking his revolver to the brute?" Perhaps I said "no officer," but it didn't matter; my tone was offensive and my attitude was potentially fatal. Yet I always behaved as if among friends, as if I could sway everyone over to my cause.

Ironically, once I had arrived in Tunis, I went to see Bürklin, recovering from his wounds. He could hardly speak, but he warned me that war in the open desert was a different thing from any I had known. "Watch out—for—low-flying—enemy aircraft," he said. "They have so many planes they can use a whole squadron"—he gasped with cumulative discomfort—"to attack a single vehicle." I had promised to keep my eyes and ears wide open, but desert warfare was even more than he had said, requiring a different phase of operations each day, today an attack, tomorrow defense, then a withdrawal, then attack again, then a delaying action perhaps. "In one fortnight," I told Broich, "you put into action everything you learned in Staff College."

The end of the Tunisian campaign was already close at hand, and Broich agreed with me that I should be flown back to Italy and thence home to Germany, where I might be of use. I was fit, had lost weight, and so was slimmer and seemed even taller than usual; a luxury-loving, renegade part of me longed for the ocean in the Gulf of Gabès, due east of Gafsa. Well, if not that, then *any* ocean. First, though, I had to do my own share in the so-called withdrawal and delaying action. Since the Allies had complete air superiority, a divisional commander and his chief of staff did not travel in the same vehicle. I went first, to set up the new command post, farther back, and Broich told me "Look out for aircraft. I will follow in about an hour, once the last battalion has come through." Off I went. It was April 7th, and much too clear to be moving about on the sand.

I wish I could say that I noticed something like a silver salmon, carving hot-fanged out of the innocent sky, but all I saw was a slab of pale brown wafting over me as the plane made a low pass, then banked at no altitude at all, and came back firing right at my car in parallel multiple furrows that raced toward us and, instead of passing us by on either side, cut right through. Was it a mine as well, I dizzily wondered before a black sluice out of nowhere rolled down my face and I toppled after it into a clanking iron pan. At the main dressing station they amputated my right hand above the wrist, and the third and fourth fingers of my left hand. They also removed what was left of my left eye. My left ear was injured, as was my left knee, although these were minor troubles by comparison.

For three days I lay in a coma, under those scalding azure skies. Then I was transferred to hospital in Carthage, as much dead as alive, and almost certain to be totally blind even if I survived. Back in the desert, Broich had tried to cross an open plain with only a wireless truck and two dispatch riders, and twenty fighters had attacked them. Yet they escaped to find, not far ahead, my own vehicle riddled with holes. I little knew then that the one attack, the one on me, would trigger an attack of my own, on a target much more imperative than ever I could be.

6

To Carthage, then, I came, able only to murmur to my mind's ear, *Stauffenberg delendus est.* Stauffenberg is to be destroyed, but not *deletus est,* which would mean my destruction had already taken place. The city was intact, ironically enough. Someone with a sense of humor told me so. I certainly could not have established the fact for myself. I mumbled away about the Punic Wars, Roman sea power, the bizarre language of the Phoenicians, and Dido herself with a willow wand in her grasp, trying to bring her true love home again. I was nothing if not the classical scholar finally on home ground. Imagine: to convalesce—no, to come back to life—in so fabled, so resonant a place, somehow reinforced my sense of being among the elect. I knew I would survive, although in what deformed shape I could not tell. Praying to and for me from the depths of the slow-mounting spring in the German countryside, my Nina was far from ready for widow's weeds. The pain had a roaring, sucking plunge that dwindled to a feather-tickle, which then became a comb of needles stroked across my nerves. The empty eye tugged the length of my body at my knee, which vibrated in my wrist and in the thumb and two remaining fingers of my other hand. So much of what one is, after water, is raw meat, and I was never so conscious of the fact. It helped not at all to know that Leibnitz (my battle reading) had said that only God is completely without body, and that the births and deaths of natural bodies are not abrupt transitions but gradual changes.

Only God, he wrote in his knowledgeable way, is an uncreated monad; all else is created or derivative, in accordance with a process he named "fulguration." Well, I had just been "fulgurated," and my Latin told me the word meant hit by lightning. *Fulgurator* meant an interpreter of lightning. It would have been gross if the low-flying plane had been a Lockheed *Lightning*, but I heard distant murmurs to the effect that it had been a Hurricane or a Spitfire (someone's aircraft-recognition was rather sloppy, but who cared?). What seemed to me astonishing was that, almost as if in parody of Leibnitz, I had been recreated in a flash, a flash that still toured at speed inside my head, while so-called "fulguration" was God's activity continued from moment to moment. With a priest hovering to give me the last rites, I was actually under other auspices: well, if not other, at least higher up the chain of command, and I thought, quite without vainglorious whims, I had been tested in the flame, saved for a purpose. This thing had not happened for nothing. I realize now that one can impose whatever significance one wishes and events do not resist; but my sense of things there in Carthage was not so much that I had been chosen as that, having begun to pull through, I must never waste what was left—both of and to me. I felt a new vigor invading but not displacing the pain, like heat moving into mercury in a hair-fine tube. At death's door, I drew back the hand that made as if to knock and turned my spoiled face back toward the thought: *me, now.*

SEVEN POEMS

PETER BALAKIAN

REPLY FROM WILDERNESS ISLAND

I want the eye of the fish to turn
in the black water
and catch the sun of my hook.

For the fish enters my dream with
a smooth fin for my face.

•

I want the tail of the fish
to turn inside my muscle
and travel my spine as it would the rushing stream.

For the fish enters my dream
with a sheen of scales changing in the light.

•

I want the fin of the fish to wriggle
its fine web in the dark center of my chest

turning all blood from water to a pool that covers rock.

For the fish enters my dream
with green gills and a ruby-stained belly.

WINTER REVIVAL

Ice is imagined
as insulation from frostbite.
Gangrene is prevented
by the thighs.
Your tongue holds
the month,
curls the weather
with its vermicular
underlining
and returns heat
blue to the throat.

The night is exhaled.
Each breath
and another degree
approaches zero:
the center hard
with substance that moves
to fluid near light–
a circle with an ocean
frozen at bottom.

The white of the eye
has a light of its own.
You can even fish
in its clear pool.
Drop the hook
beneath the thin
frozen lip
and wait patiently–

the line slipping
through your hands,
wind stinging the ears
crimson along a rim
of boney cartilage.

The flesh wrinkles
like hide,
hardens like the skin
of a lizard:

even a knife-point
three inches deep
can only be seen
with the eyes.

READING THROUGH ICE

Wake with sun
and the sill will be sealed
with a band of ice;
too smooth to cut your wrists on,
long enough to plunge
down your throat
and break the first sound loose.

A thin sheet of ice
is a bifocal.
You read the morning headlines
through the air bubbles
that are trapped in the clear distance
like the monotone thump from the heart
that separates its echo
from your voice
until the groundhog runs
scared of its shadow.

The ice junkie bottles his fluid innards
and packs his skin to the gutter.
Geese prepare for each wind
by circling the white sky
and shortening their glide.
Use an icicle as a hypodermic,
and when it melts
you'll feel your hands
peel your lips from the pane.

This morning you realize
how little the river reflects;
how even the branches of oak
are thin and gray at top.
If you sing a song next to the bark
each limb will crack
and scavenging squirrels will
crawl from the trunks
and burrow holes
in your map of Alaska.

THREE LANDSCAPES IN MOTION

It happens like this;
a sagging willow brushes
the top of your head.
The ground like a strange
foil shines.
You move by waist
through high grass.

You take the dry weeds
and use them for arms.

•

A stream thinner than your wrist
dries at your feet.
Red clay cracks
like the skin
of the lizard's lips.
The sun withers to
an orange arm.
You want to follow it out

you remember
the other side of sky
is cold as the rock
that sends a breeze
to your face.

•

It happens like this;
sky lowers to your ears,
you find the bay
entering your mouth.
Small bait and weed
run the passage of your nose
and return to wave.

You recognize the far shore
as a wide belly of fish;
the near jetty
as black fin.

POEM FOR A NEW FISH

From Equinox
a Pentecost is past.
The sun's movement visible
once more from a position

fixed in the mind.
The sun
if it rotates in your sleep
still recedes
to a single point
where the earth's
open eye
becomes your own.
The arc you draw
from a shore point
is the azimuth
marked by the pupil.

In a week there will
be more undertoe,
the small bones
in the foot will bow.
You can almost predict
the flight
of the albatross
over the antarctic–
the span of wing
over ice.
Each wave diminishing
with the size
of your pupil,
the water dropping
to where your ankles
leave the air.

•

Let your foot
follow the current.
The thin membrane
of jellyfish
will widen the pores.
Imagine yourself sinking
into the den of China.

Admit that the sand
packs the memory
hard to the heelskin,
the minimal arch bunches
the unknown to a cold
bone, the rest passes
through a fearless tibia.

Salt dries
on your leg hair,
a calendar drops
from a plane
flying advertising.
The ocean dissolves
all the waste
you can imagine.
Last night you came
here to piss,
dropped your trunks
and let the salt
find its way
through the pubic hair
to your skin.
Your penis wriggled
like a fish just hatched
the salt water washed
the inland dryness
out of your bowels.
China was itself again
and the moon
August orange
spoked a light
a hop, skip
and a jump
to a vanishing point
beyond your arm.

THE FIELD OF POPPIES

for Lu

Cypress spiral to the sky.
Painters came here because
the dirt was dry as their bones,
because even the monastery on the hill
flaked each day.
You want a picture of yourself
in this poppy field;
wind blowing the long grass
around your legs,
fields of yellow flower across
the road moving away from you.
The high mountain is where
the town's saint disappeared
with his wound.
When he returned
peach trees sprouted from rock,
and the gray clouds left the mountain.

Cypress spiral to the sky.
Your father found this field
and the mountain uncovered,
the monastery a pure glint of sun.
You want this picture
to show your body disappearing
in the red waves of flower,
a field of pin-pricks
rising and falling in the breeze,
each step spreading the red
over your joints.

You want the red to cover
the mountain,
you want the line where
sky and land meet
to turn the color of the heart.

This is how your father left;
foot, knee, stomach, face
disappearing in the stain of this field,
in the light wind that sang
in the red flowers.

HOMAGE TO HART CRANE

This morning kelp is drying on the dockside,
women leave the laundromat early.
I walk the low bank
in the low air
and feel the long bones in the river's belly
hiss in the warming water.
How many warmings of current wound through
your eyes Hart Crane?
This morning your dry rib
passes this juncture of ocean and calm.
Here where there's no bridge
and gulls roost on tied barges
and skim the black harbor for carp,
your marrow goes the way of slow mollusks.

The sun moves
in a steady progression upwards
to a point
for a fraction of light
before it starts to fall
and here, Hart Crane
even the falling warehouses
look like cathedrals for a moment.

This morning a drunken fisherman
wakes on cinder with dead bait in his hand,
not knowing the day of week
the month or year,

not knowing anything
but the spot he sees the sun in,
the noon wind riveting his ribs.

It's a good thing, Hart Crane
that I'm baitless and hookless
that I leave the bay without a fish,
my net shredded and hanging on the old post at the South Dock.
It's a good thing my girl took the first train south
and that this noon I unwrap my sandwich alone
under the empty elm, with three birds singing in my ears
and the cats meowing over empty clam shells and shrimp husks.

What luck Hart Crane
that I came this morning to feel your one bone
dragging along the bottom
just as the sun was climbing to the top
and the fisherman was waking,
just as the tugs were disappearing
and the barges were settling in
to the winter lapping of the harbor,
just as the cod heads were softening around the eye
so the gulls could snap them up.

THE INVESTIGATION

PETER KURINSKY

I do not often speak my mind. I often feel that there is little I have to say. There are days in fact when I do not open my mouth to utter a syllable, much less to say something substantial. I do not consider myself an articulate or even a very intelligent man. I was a poor student in school and I am at present a social failure. I must admit that I have never before written a story, yet I feel at this time compelled to summon whatever aptitude I have for storytelling, however small, in order to set my mind at peace about a certain incident, or rather series of incidents, that befell me some time ago, and the memory of which still haunts my every moment, both waking and sleeping. I have searched my mind for every last detail concerning this affair, and when my memory has failed me I have relied upon the memories and impressions of others. I do not promise that my story will be of any significant interest, yet my purpose is not to enlighten or entertain, but rather to free myself of some powerful emotions that have accompanied my thoughts, my constant deep thoughts, about this subject.

As I am a novice at this sort of thing I will make no attempt at reasonable or "artistic" organization of the facts I wish to present, or at rendering a realistic picture. The facts will be presented as they surface in the mind.

It seems natural to begin, as they say, at the beginning. But as I have a choice of which beginning at which I will begin, for there are in life many beginnings, in order to present a full picture I suppose I would do best to begin at the very beginning, my own beginning, the circumstances of my birth.

The story goes that there were four gentlemen present at my birth: my father, and three of his friends—a Mr. Stein, a Mr. Delvaux, and a Mr. Alvarez. It is said that on the occasion of my mother's becoming pregnant with me, her first and only child, these gentlemen, all of whom, with the exception of Mr. Alvarez, were respectable men of high positions (I shall get to Mr. Alvarez later), had a high time trying to guess of which sex the child would be, and that in the course of their speculations on this issue it occurred to one of them, Mr. Alvarez, who was well known to be a gambler, that it might not be a bad idea to wager money on their respective speculations, and thereby to raise the level of their argument to a financial venture. I have been told that my father at first opposed this idea, that to him it seemed somehow out of place to put bets on an unborn baby, and that such an enterprise would be an insult not only to his wife and to himself but to the nature of birth in general. But on consulting his wife, my mother, it was decided to go ahead with the wager. My mother herself placed ten dollars on my being a boy, and in time the game aroused the interest of the whole village of Belville. On the day of my birth there were said to be many people gathered outside the hospital, waiting for the result, myself, and when I finally made my appearance in the world, there was much excitement on the part of about half the population of the town, and a general lowering of the spirits of the others. Among my souvenirs I have a copy of the local newspaper of the next morning, with a headline reading: "It's a Boy!" My father is said to have lost a good two thousand dollars on his conviction that his newborn baby would be a girl, as he had desired.

Lest the reader think that I am somehow exaggerating my story in order to gain sympathy or interest, I am exaggerating nothing. I am telling it just as I heard it.

From the start, it could be said, I brought unhappiness to my father. Whether or not my sex at birth is accountable for the lack of interest I was to feel he had in me, I cannot say. But it is a fact that to this very day my father refers to me as "The Error." When my mother and father divorced, shortly after my twelfth birthday, there was no question but that I would remain in the custody of my mother, as I had always been, in effect, her child and not my father's.

So my lack of confidence in myself, my feeling that I am always inadequate, can be traced to the very beginning. There is no doubt in my mind that I am made of an inferior substance. This conviction is supported, time and again, by the dreadful errors I make in my daily life—errors which to me are as natural as positive accomplishments are to a more fortunate fellow. Since childhood I have known that the people around me have considered me foolish and incompetent. Not a day passes when I am not made more aware of my basic inferiority in some form or other. Simple encounters which would not even seem to hold the potential for failure or humiliation are somehow endowed with new possibilities, when I am involved. Clerks, cashiers, waitresses, and postmen find in me a wealth of things to dislike. Yet when I try to ask myself just what it is in me that they find so dislikable, I come up with nothing. My appearance is unextraordinary, and my manners of speech and dress are normal. Unless there is something I am not aware of—as the truly stupid are not conscious of their stupidity—I do not know how I differ from other people. It was this line of thinking that led me to believe that perhaps other people know something about me that I don't know. All throughout school I was preoccupied with this belief. In everyone's eyes I saw the confirmation of this belief. Therefore I kept to myself, and I did not make friends. As a result my schoolwork suffered. It was only by the skin of my teeth, as they say, that I passed my courses.

My work as an insurance claims adjustor is simple and there is not much room for mistakes, but my expectation of failure is now incorporated into nearly everything else that I try to do. Whereas, when still a boy, under my father's hand, I was made to feel the gravity of my failure only after the act, so to speak, and whereas as a young man I myself became aware of my failure only after many attempts to prove myself worthy, now it seems increasingly futile even to make an attempt. When I say attempt I suppose I am thinking of Mary. I had not planned on bringing this incident to light, but as my purpose is to express the full truth about myself, I guess that now is as good a time as ever to talk about it.

Mary worked as a secretary to the small insurance firm in which

I was first employed as claims adjustor. Our relationship, if one can call it that, spanned a period of about two months. I feel a reluctance to discuss it. Her name, as I have said, was Mary, I believe. Sometimes she called herself Mary and sometimes Marie. This was but one of her many affectations. Others included a tendency to avert her eyes whenever one spoke to her, as if she could not hear, to feign indifference, or to ignore one completely.

I first felt the stirrings of what could be called love, or at least strong attraction, on the first day of my employment in that firm. My contact with Mary at that time was limited to sharing a telephone and brushing shoulders. I was enamored of the way the light played in her hair, by the fullness of her mouth and the length of her neck, even I suppose by her slightly arrogant manner. Yet she showed no trace whatsoever of any kind of interest in me.

I thought of her every moment, as much as this is possible. I am not one to generalize, but when one is under the spell of love for an individual it is difficult, nay impossible, to be reasonable and consider that individual's lack of a similar interest in oneself. Hence I, who am not one, under normal circumstances, to openly express lesser feelings, found myself going to great lengths to gain her attention, and ultimately, her affection.

My attempts, need I say it, failed. Not only did they fail but they had quite the reverse effect of what I desired. With each offer to walk her home, to open her mail for her, to buy her lunch, to decipher legal documents which only the person educated in these things can read, I sensed a further degree of alienation, not merely from her but from other of my coworkers who had apparently been informed of my antics.

Finally she put me in my place: "Alexander," she said, "if this is the way that you were taught to treat women, if you think you can gain my favor by striking blows to my competency and my independence, then I wonder how you were raised. You must have hated your mother. You obviously hate women if you think that this kind of behavior—behavior which embarrasses not only you but me, and everyone in the office—will impress me. You are a fool, Alexander. Now leave me alone."

I am still trying to recover from this incident. I was forced to leave that office and seek employment elsewhere.

There, I have said it. It is amazing how writing something down can have such a purging effect. But there is more to come.

I do not blame my parents for how I turned out. I hold myself responsible. However, I do hold them responsible for being a part to a particular insult to my character, which will be mentioned in due course.

An intense curiosity about how I came to be how I am led me on an investigation which lasted several months. During this time I wished to ascertain a suspicion that I had had for years previous, and which was not based so much on tangible fact but on a feeling, a deep-rooted feeling, that there was something questionable in my past, that people around me knew something that I did not know . . .

In trying to research my early years I came upon considerable resistance on the part of my mother even to speak of those days, and my own memories of my boyhood are so faint and insubstantial as to be worthless. So it was that I found reason to contact one Jeanette Arthur, the woman who had served as housekeeper to my mother, in the house in Belville, during my early life. Finding this woman was no easy task. Rumor had it that she had long ago moved out of Belville into the countryside, yet attempts at locating her proved fruitless. It was quite by accident, as a matter of fact, that I came upon her house on a walk through the village of Montrouge, deep in the mountains, on a brief holiday. Of course the name Arthur is not uncommon in our parts, yet I put aside this consideration and knocked on her door. Something told me that I would find her inside.

I have said that I have little memory of my childhood, yet when Mrs. Arthur came to the door, and I got a good look at her face, I felt an immediate shock of recognition. Certainly she had aged, but very gracefully. She was now in her mid-sixties, I estimated, and she spoke in a deep voice which was oddly familiar to me. At first she did not recognize me, but she invited me inside, yet not without inquiring first as to the purpose of my visit:

"They have advised us to lock all the doors and not to admit strangers," she explained. "Apparently there is some lunatic on the loose and he has already broken into three houses in this neighborhood. But Alexander! Do come in! I know it is funny to say but I have almost been expecting you."

"How is that, Mrs. Arthur?" I asked, somewhat taken aback. We had not seen each other for over twenty years.

"Oh, I am a great believer in the occult and extrasensory perception. Things like that," she explained. "Now sit down and I'll make some tea. My how you've grown! But that is foolish of me. You are a grown man now. What a pleasure to see you!"

Mrs. Arthur, I soon learned, played an important part in my childhood—more important, perhaps, than my own mother. In the course of our discussion over tea and small cakes, I soon realized why my mother had been reluctant to speak of my first five years. It seems that due to other involvements she was unable to attend to to me those first five years, and that Mrs. Arthur was therefore hired not as a housekeeper, as I had been told, but as a nanny. She alone had been responsible for me. This is not to say that my parents had no part in my upbringing—on the contrary.

"Your father," recalled Mrs. Arthur, "was a very severe disciplinarian. As a result you were always scared of him. You would always cry whenever he got near you, and this made him extremely angry. I remember the time I was forced to leave for a few days to visit a sick sister. I was only gone a few days, but when I got back you ran into my arms and cried. It seems that you had been so terrified of your father that you refused to eat for three days, and they had to force-feed you."

"Why do you suppose he treated me so badly, Mrs. Arthur?" I asked. "Was it something I did?"

"I cannot say, Alexander. Perhaps it was just his nature."

"And what of my mother? What was keeping her so busy that she had no time to take care of me?"

"I'm afraid that," she said, "will have to remain my secret. As much as I appreciate your curiosity, I made a vow to your mother at the time, and I am not one to break promises."

"But certainly you can tell me something," I said. "What was it? Another man? You must see that I am entitled to this information. The vow that you made to my mother can certainly be broken now. After all, twenty years have passed and it should make no difference to her now. Anyhow, she will never get wind that you have told me."

"You must realize, Alexander," she replied severely, "that I am a very superstitious woman. There are certain things that I believe should never be tampered with."

"I believe you are being ridiculous, Mrs. Arthur," I told her, however this statement seems a little rash in retrospect.

"If the information is important enough to you, Alexander," she replied with a stern and serious tone, "then it will come to you in some form or another, if you look for it. I am not going to be the one to reveal it to you. I have invited you into my home, we have had tea together, and we have shared memories. If I had known that you were going to pry into affairs that have been long buried and that should not be unearthed, then perhaps I would not have let you in at all. Now I must get back to what I was doing before you came. I hate to ask you to leave, but if that is what it is going to take . . ."

"No, you needn't ask me to leave," I said. "I am grateful for what you have told me so far, and I beg your forgiveness for my impertinence. Good day, Mrs. Arthur."

Mrs. Arthur was to be of some importance to subsequent events. I had no intention of leaving things as they were, and I was to visit her home several more times.

Lest the reader think that I am straying from my original purpose, I am doing nothing of the kind. All things will add up in the end. Nothing, in this story, is irrelevant.

Perhaps it is best to explain some more about my reasons for conducting this investigation of my past. I have already mentioned that my father has always had little regard for me, that he openly displayed his animosity toward me. He never had a kind word to say about me. I saw nothing of him after his divorce from my mother, when I was twelve. All I heard about him, when I made inquiries to my mother, were negative remarks, suggesting in effect that my father was a scoundrel, a "miserable no-good wretch," as she called him, yet never had I been told of just what he had done to deserve such names. Upon pressing my mother further, she would tell me nothing, and she advised me to leave the matter closed. But it is important for a young man to have a knowledge of his father. It contributes to his own sense of manhood. So it was mainly out of curiosity about my father that I undertook my investigation, but in the process I have learned perhaps more than it is good for me to know.

As my mother was of no use to me in my investigation, and Mrs. Arthur's mouth was firmly closed on the subject, I found myself temporarily at a loss to know just how to proceed further. Questioning of people involved only peripherally in my upbringing, such as doctors and tutors, produced nothing. However, during my interviews with these people I became increasingly confident that I was indeed correct in my suspicion that these people's silence was not due merely to defective memories or unwillingness to get involved, but rather of secret information which to their thinking should not be revealed. In all cases there was the same look of secrecy, the same confounded obstinacy. "No," was a common response, "I remember nothing of those days. Absolutely nothing. You will have to go elsewhere for your information. I will tell you nothing, Alexander."

Repeated disappointments led me back to the house of Mrs. Arthur.

"You are wasting your time, Alexander," she told me. "It was my mistake to even tell you that there is something worth knowing. You must relax and put aside this investigation of yours. It will lead you nowhere. You will get yourself into trouble. I have informed your mother of what you are up to. She is gravely concerned, Alexander."

"My mother? But you have no right to tell my mother anything! By what right do you interfere with my private life, Mrs. Arthur? I am a grown man, Mrs. Arthur, and I can watch out for myself!"

"Relax, Alexander, relax," she said. "You are making a mountain out of a molehill. You will cause nothing but trouble for yourself and your family. I urge you to please abandon your investigation and go on with your life. There is no sense in trying to dig up the past. It is buried! Leave it that way."

Needless to say I did nothing of the kind. Mrs. Arthur's admonition did nothing but strengthen my determination to get to the bottom of the whole business. And since she would not help me I then decided to go directly to my mother.

It is important to explain that my mother was not in the best of health at the time of my visit to her. She had once been a strong and vital woman of unusual energy, yet from the time of her divorce, when I was twelve, her emotional stability had steadily deteriorated, she was prone to all variety of nervous conditions, and she had most recently been under the care of a prominent psychiatrist. I should mention that after the divorce I remained with her for no more than a year and a half, during which, to the best of my memory, we had a splendid and close relationship. However, when I turned thirteen I was packed off to boardingschool in the country, and hence I did not see her but for infrequent vacations and weekend visits. During the four years of boardingschool I had much reason to be concerned about her. With each visit she seemed all the more unhappy and nervous; yet she tried always to maintain a façade of contentment. After boardingschool I went directly to the university, and from the university to my first position as insurance claims adjustor with a small firm in a village far from Belville, so I had virtually lost all contact with her, and it is only in connection with my investigation that I saw her again, upon my appointment to a firm in the vicinity of Belville.

Now that I think of it, it may well have been my investigative work as a claims adjustor, my developing taste for detective work, that was responsible for my passion to look into my own past. Investigating small fires and stolen jewelry is fine, but one soon develops a taste for the larger mysteries, especially when they concern oneself. Since boyhood I had always been troubled by a deep feeling of inferiority, as I have already mentioned. Readings in psychiatric literature aroused my interest in the relationship of my childhood to the present. Often it happens, I had heard, that an early childhood experience can have a very profound effect on a person's entire life. Normally a person would enlist the services of a qualified professional analyst, yet this did not interest me. I have already said that I am a shy, reserved man. I simply do not like to talk. To be perfectly honest I did visit an analyst, once. But during the course of the session my lips did not move, even slightly. I sat during the session like a criminal who does not wish to incriminate himself. And the doctor himself, as I understand to be the manner of many of these doctors, behaved similarly; he too said nothing, and I left in a state of severe disorientation.

To get back to my mother, I must explain that her condition during my visits was of a highly emotional caliber, so that one must not take what I am about to describe as being too true a reflection of her real character or personality. I will defend my mother to the end. That she found herself in circumstances beyond her control cannot be considered her fault. But I am running ahead of myself. I must admit to the reader that what I am about to describe, a brief but highly charged scene, causes me considerable anguish each time I think of it, and I think of it often, perhaps too often for my own peace of mind. It was the first of only two visits, separated in time by approximately two months, and it lasted no more than half an hour. Yet in that half hour, the first of two, the scales could be said to have fallen, if only partially, from my eyes. It was a half hour that will have a very profound influence on the rest of my life.

I did not call before appearing at my mother's door. It was a Wednesday. I remember it well. The skies were blue. I remember this well because I remember being quite awe-struck by the beauty of the day. My mother's house in Belville sits atop a large hill overgrown with moss and vines. One has to pass first through a small forest of large trees, up a path made of pebbles. Only then does one begin to approach the house. My memory of the house was nothing in comparison with the real thing. Made of stone, it is four stories high, and it has the character of one of those houses in the story books, although it is possible that my emotional attachment to the house in which I was raised makes me romanticize things slightly. Suffice it to say that the house is considered one of the finest in all of Belville, and although the grounds have been badly neglected over the years, it still gives one the impression of grandeur and good taste.

I rang the bell and wes met at the door by a servant, a young man.

"I wish to see Mrs. Remick," I said.

"Who can I say is calling?" he asked.

"I am her son, Alexander."

The young man, at first, looked a little suspicious. This was understandable to me. I must remind the reader that I had not been back at the house for nearly twelve years. My communications with my mother were, previous to this day, all conducted over the telephone, and in those phone calls I had gotten the distinct impression that she did not wish to see me. Although she never actually told me so, one can detect these things from a tone of voice.

So the servant, the young man, had most likely never heard of me before, or if he had he had most likely heard that my mother did not wish to see me. And furthermore, he probably thought, how can I be sure that this is not some intruder who is using Alexander's name in order to gain entrance to the house? Finally I was prompted to show him several documents of identification which I had brought with me for this purpose, and then he admitted me past the door and into a parlor where I was to wait.

The feeling I had on returning to my childhood home was almost comparable to an actual regression in time. For a moment I felt a bit dazed, as if under the influence of some kind of liquor. Then it occurred to me that this must certainly be a dream. Things took on a slightly unnatural air. The sight of a lamp which I remembered distinctly from childhood had the impact of jarring me from the present. A particular chair inspired a plethora of emotions and memories. But in a moment I had regained my composure and my grasp of reality, and I sat down and waited.

My mother appeared nearly forty minutes later, and she was obviously upset.

"You have no business coming here, Alexander," she told me. "You might have at least called first. I am totally unprepared for your visit. As a matter of fact I am expecting other guests. You can only stay a few minutes."

"Aren't you pleased to see me, your own son?" I asked with annoyance. "After all, Mother, we have not seen each other in years. You may not be pleased to see me but at least you could put up some kind of façade of surprise, or at least the smallest pleasure in seeing me again."

Then, as I remember it, she lit a cigarette and began to smoke it feverishly. "I have heard, Alexander, what you are up to, and I don't approve . . . to say the least. To go around asking questions about my past is not my idea of respect for your mother. The least you might have done is to tell me what you were up to. Good God, it gives me shivers to think that my own son is involved in a conspiracy to ruin my name and reputation! What, Alexander . . . what, I ask you . . . what have I done to deserve such abuse? A woman does all she can to make a good home for her son, she gives him everything he wants, she sends him to the finest school, and what is her reward? One day she picks up the telephone and a housekeeper from twenty years ago tells her that her son is conducting an investigation—an investigation, that was her word—of his past, that he is going all over the countryside looking for dirt about his mother, that he will stop at nothing. Is this the way to treat a woman in my condition? Is it your purpose, Alexander, to give your mother a heart attack? Well, if that is what you want to do, my boy, then I won't stop you. You can shout it from the roof-tops for all I care, Alexander. You can post it all over town! Are you short for money? I'll pay for it, no less. I'll pay for it! How much do you want? One thousand? Two thousand? Erickson!" she called to the young man who was still standing by the door with a bemused look on his face. "Get me my checkbook. My son wants me to finance a plot to destroy me."

I tried to reason with her. I asked her to please sit down, to allow me to explain. I tried to explain that she had it all wrong, that she was confusing things, but she would not listen. In a moment her hysteria had turned into a flood of tears:

"My own boy," she cried. "My own little Alexander. Who would have thought? Such a sweet child! Who could ask for a sweeter child? Oh, Alexander, if only you knew. If only you knew what heartache you have caused your mother . . . I sit here all day long. I ask myself: Where did you go wrong? What could you have done to deserve such an ungrateful son? This is my reward for years of sacrifice. My boy, let me try to talk you out of it. What do you want from me? Money? I will give you all you want. Your mother is weak, Alexander. The doctor says that too severe a shock could send her over the edge. I must beg you, Alexander, to think this thing out. Talk to your mother. Tell me about yourself. Come closer. Mother won't bite."

From a short distance away, my mother could easily pass for a woman of twenty-five or thirty. Her figure is slim, her black hair well coiffed, and her clothes carefully chosen. In her appearance and her manner she maintains a dignity and poise which mark her as a woman of good breeding and class. In her earlier years she had always been considered one of the most beautiful women in all of Belville. She was admired and envied by many less fortunate women.

Yet upon closer examination my mother was clearly neither young in years nor in spirit. Years of unhappiness were evident in her face. Heavily applied make-up did little to conceal the trouble she had known. Her eyes were sunken and her entire face etched with little lines. Yes, on closer examination my mother looked far older than her fifty-odd years. When she spoke to me her eyes filled with tears, and her lips quivered. I could hardly keep myself from crying.

"Your mother," she said in a trembling voice, "is very ill, Alexander. The doctor says . . ."

"Please, Mother," I said, taking her hand into mine. "I do not mean to upset you. If I had known that this business would upset you so I would never have started anything. But you must understand that a person is entitled to a knowledge of his background. I have always felt that there was something being kept from me. You must know that the people of Belville have no respect for me, that I can hardly pass someone on the street without getting some kind of a look. It has always been this way. I have asked myself: Is it your appearance, Alexander? Is there something strange in the way you walk? Is there something unusual about your face? But look at me, Mother! This is a normal face, wouldn't you say? Not a handsome face, mind you, but a normal face?"

"Very normal," she responded, doing nothing to hold back the tears. "A pleasant face, now that I look at you. I can see your father's eyes. Yes, you have your father's eyes. There is no doubt about it."

"Do you know that I can hardly go into a store to buy a cigar without feeling that even the girl behind the counter knows something about me that I don't know . . ."

"But it is all in your imagination, Alexander. Nobody is trying to hurt you. Everybody loves you."

"No, Mother! That is not the way it is at all! People laugh at me wherever I go. I can sense it. They make fun of everything I do! You must help me to get to the root of it!"

"Now you are going too far, Alexander. I will have to ask you to leave. If you don't leave of your own accord I will have Erickson throw you out. You are upsetting me." At this she removed her hand from mine, rose from her chair, and turned her back to me. I considered for a moment that perhaps I ought not to pursue the matter any further. The reader must believe that I did not wish to upset my mother, that was not my purpose at all. Yet my determination to get to the bottom of the matter, and increasingly I was sure that there was something important being concealed from me, outweighed my apprehension.

"I will not leave until you tell me why you were never at home during my first five years, why I was put in the care of Mrs. Arthur, and precisely why my father always hated me. I will not leave until I get some answers. I will sit right here in this chair until tomorrow, if necessary. I realize your dilemma, Mother. If you tell me you will not only betray yourself and my father but whoever else was involved."

For at least a minute there was nothing but silence. My mother did not move. Then in a tearful cracked voice she called for Erickson.

"Erickson! My son Alexander would like to leave now!"

Lest the reader think that I was willing to destroy my own mother in the process of discovering the secret, I must say that that could not be further from the truth. During the weeks that followed the previously described incident, I could not sleep at night. However hard I tried to think of other things, my thoughts always returned to my mother and the anguish I had caused her. As a result my health suffered. I had difficulty swallowing food. I paced every night until two in the morning, sometimes later. I became more and more obsessed by the idea that the whole world knew something about me that I did not know, and for days I would not even go out on the street in fear of encountering a friend of the family or a relation. It could almost be said that I became convinced that my crime was written all over my face, that it was visible to all the world—all the world, that is, except myself.

Frequently I called my mother's house and asked to talk to her. "Your mother," Erickson told me time and again, "is not feeling well. Haven't you done enough to upset her? Leave her alone."

I called Mrs. Arthur in the country: "Alexander, you are wasting your time. Your mother is an emotional wreck. The doctor says that she is heading toward another collapse. She has called me several times and begged me not to talk to you any longer. She is like a madwoman. Give it up, Alexander, and leave the area. The cards tell me that you will come to no good if you remain near Belville, and the cards do not lie. For your own sake, for your mother's sake, for my sake, please stop this nonsense."

I stayed in my room for weeks. I myself became like a madman. I talked to no one. I went out only for food. There were times, I must admit, when I almost felt that I had lost control of myself, that I was living out some strange dream. I remember standing in front of the mirror and asking myself: "Why are you doing this to yourself? You should listen to them. You should leave well enough alone and move away from here." But in a sense I had lost control. With each passing day I became more determined. I remembered Mrs. Arthur's advice: "If it is important enough to you, the secret will come to you."

Then one day a letter arrived in the mail. It bore no signature and it said simply: "If you are determined to dig up the past then perhaps I can be of assistance to you. Meet me at the Café de la Grass on Wednesday the ninth at noon."

The Café de la Grass is located a good mile outside of the center of Belville. It is noted for its fine French cuisine and one can eat there only by reservation. Whoever had summoned me was wise enough to consider that we meet in a private place. When I tried to think of who it might have been, I could think of no one but my father. Conceivably my mother had contacted him about my investigation. To be perfectly honest I had a strong hope that my accomplice would in fact turn out to be my father. As much as I had always feared him, this was outweighed by an intense curiosity to see him face to face after so many years, to talk with him, and perhaps even to express my resentment toward him with some of my new-found courage. Yet the idea of actually meeting him scared me, and for a moment I thought that perhaps the whole thing was getting out of hand. What would happen if he had a gun and wanted to kill me? But I managed to calm down, telling myself that my imagination was playing tricks on me, and I appeared at the appointed time.

At 12:05 precisely, a tall figure dressed in a long black coat entered the room. As he removed his coat and handed it to the maître d', I thought that surely this was my father. When he approached the table there was hardly a doubt in my mind. You see I had no photographs of my father. My mother had forbidden any in the house after their divorce, and my memory of what he had looked like was dim.

I was numb with fear, but I stood and projected out my hand in timorous greeting.

"Good day, Alexander," he said. "My name is Thomas Alvarez."

I did not respond to his greeting. Instead I merely let go his hand and stood in amazement. Here was the man who had reduced the day of my birth to a carnival. I had never seen him before, and I had no desire to see him now. I felt myself blush and begin to perspire. His face, on the contrary, betrayed nothing but sheer amusement. Fortunately I had the good sense to restrain myself from giving in to an impulse to punch him.

Finally I forced myself to talk: "I do not wish to have lunch with you, Mr. Alvarez," I said, and I turned to leave.

"But Alexander, I can be of help to you. Please, sit down. It will only take a few minutes. I have heard that you are making inquiries into your past, that you have gotten it into your head that there is something you are entitled to know that no one has told you. Well, you are right."

As a waiter was approaching to take our order, Mr. Alvarez paused. I told him to come back in a few minutes and Alvarez resumed:

"And I am in a position to tell you just what it is, for a price."

"A price? What do you mean, a price?"

"I will tell you all you want to know, and believe me there is plenty, for a sum of three thousand dollars, no less, and on the condition that you tell no one that I was the one to tell you. Otherwise your mother would be extremely angry with both of us, and we wouldn't want that, would we?"

"There is no way, Mr. Alvarez," I told him, "that I will pay you three thousand dollars for information that has nothing to do with you."

"But that is exactly the point, Alexander. It has everything to do with me and it is only from me that you will ever hear it. Your mother would die before she would admit it to you, and your father will not even speak to you. Now be reasonable, Alexander. It seems to me a very reasonable amount."

"I will not do it," I insisted.

"This is your only chance, Alexander," he said.

"Well then so be it. I will pay you nothing. Now good day."

Anyone but an idiot could make a simple deduction from this conversation as to what the secret might have been. I myself made the very same deduction. Needless to say I was extremely upset about the implication of Alvarez's offer. In all my thinking about what the secret might have been, it did not once occur to me that my father's hostility toward me might have been due to his not being my real father; and certainly even if that were true it would never have dawned on me that my real father was Thomas Alvarez. I returned to my room and spent the following several weeks alone, trying to think things out.

I must admit that during those weeks in my room I must have become steadily more confused and upset. I have no recollection of eating anything during those days, but certainly I must have eaten something or else I would not have survived to tell about it. Often I thought of calling Alvarez and giving him the money. But I had the good sense to decide that if I was going to be told the secret, it was not going to be by the likes of Alvarez. And if my deduction were correct, why pay him the money only to hear it from his own mouth? I would have much preferred to hear it from my mother. And furthermore, if Alvarez were my real father, an idea which did not please me in the least, why then was my skin a pale white and his a darker color? Maybe he had planned on lying to me in order to get money from me. Certainly if I were his son I would bear some vague resemblance to him. I stood for hours in front of the mirror, recalling my mother's words on my last visit to her: "A pleasant face, now that I look at you. I can see your father's eyes . . . There is no doubt about it." I had seen no resemblance between my eyes and those of Alvarez.

On a windy day I packed up a few belongings, informed my landlady that I would be gone for a few days ("Where are you off to in this weather?" she asked, an amused look in her eyes), and took a train to the countryside. I knew of an inn in a small village quite near to Mrs. Arthur's house, and it was no coincidence that I chose to go there to have a few days to recuperate from my recent trauma. I would pay Mrs. Arthur one last visit, whether she liked it or not. I had a strong feeling that she would have the answer, that she would clear this whole thing up once and for all.

I spent a few pleasant days in the inn, trying to reason with myself. I told myself that even if it were true that Alvarez were my real father, this was no cause for alarm. I was still the same person. Nothing had changed. But as hard as I tried to calm myself, I was as upset as ever.

Mrs. Arthur nearly refused to allow me admittance into her house. I arrived in the dark of night. Apparently she was ill. She came to the door in her nightgown and she had a sickly pale color to her skin. Her breath gave off a nasty, sickly smell.

"Go away, Alexander, go away, I beg you. Can't you see that I am ill? You must leave me alone."

"I just want a few last words with you and then I will leave you be, Mrs. Arthur. I promise not to press you. I already know the secret. Please let me inside."

He face registered shock. "You know the secret?" she asked in disbelief. And as she closed the door behind us and led me into the parlor, she said below her breath: "It is no wonder that I have been feeling sick. The cards told me it would happen." When we were seated she rebuked me: "You should have listened to me, Alexander. I warned you, I warned you. It was an ace of spades that turned up. Very bad luck. This whole thing could have been avoided. Now we will have to read the cards again. They will tell you what to do. Oh what a mess you have made! Dear, dear . . ."

She removed a pack of ordinary playing cards from an end table drawer and laid them out on the table. As much as I insisted that I did not believe in such mysticism, I must say that something urged me to play her little game.

"You must pick four cards. It is an old mystical custom. You must pick four cards at random, and don't show them to me whatever you do. I don't want to know."

"How then will I know what they mean?"

"Well . . . It will come to you, my child. Don't worry. It will come to you."

I did as she asked. I selected four cards at random. As remarkable as it may sound, the four cards were all kings: the king of diamonds, the king of clubs, the king of hearts, and the king of spades. The reader must believe me. I am embellishing nothing. I am recording it precisely as it happened.

Despite Mrs. Arthur's insistence that I not show her the cards, I showed them to her. They had no meaning to me and I wanted to know just what they signified. And when I revealed them, her face turned a bright red.

"What do they mean?" I asked.

"Don't you know what they mean?"

"No."

"Then you must leave now, Alexander. I am not feeling well. Leave me alone. Go away." And she stood up to walk me to the door.

"I demand to know what they mean!" I shouted in frustration.

"I am tired of your demands, Alexander. You have no right to demand anything of anyone. Now leave my house at once!"

The last part of my story is the most difficult for me to write down. I have already said that the four kings had had no meaning to me whatsoever, yet I could not get them out of my mind. Then I returned to the inn, my spirits low and my mind confused, I tried to think of what to do next. I considered trying to forget everything and returning to my apartment outside of Belville. I considered going back to Mrs. Arthur's house and forcing the meaning of the cards out of her, but this would have been too cruel. I even considered, although only momentarily, the act of suicide. The reader should realize that I was not accustomed to this kind of excitement. Though I alone was responsible for what had taken place, it amazed me that in the space of two months I had managed to create such chaos. I felt almost as if I had committed murder.

All the same I went directly to my mother's house the next morning. It took everything I had in me to force myself past Erickson, to insist upon seeing my mother despite her poor health. She appeared extremely distressed when I first saw her, yet she was nevertheless still well dressed in a long purple dressing gown with little pink flowers on it, although I suppose I should mention that she was without make-up and her black hair was in disarray.

"I trust you have come to apologize, Alexander," she said while apparently studying a vase of chrysanthemums. "I will accept your apology, on the condition that I never hear another word about this so-called investigation of yours. You have hurt your mother very deeply, but I will accept your apology."

"All right, Mother. I have been thinking a great deal about it and I have come to the conclusion that no good can come from digging up the past," I said. "I have learned what I wanted to know and now I can relax."

At this point my mother's rather strained smile drooped at its edges. "What do you mean, you have learned what you wanted to know?"

"I have learned that Thomas Alvarez is my real father and that you spent my first five years with him. That is why my father never had any regard for me, and that is why the people of Belville look upon me with such contempt."

Imagine my displeasure when my mother burst into a fit of laughter.

"That is quite the funniest thing I have ever heard! So that is what you found out, is it? Who told you?"

"Alvarez himself." I saw no choice but to lie. My thinking was that if she was led to believe that I had already heard the secret from Alvarez, then she would unknowingly reveal it herself. My work as an insurance claims adjustor had taught me these little tricks of interrogation.

"Alvarez himself? Why of all the colossal nerve of that man! He must be mad! I never would have thought that he would stoop so low! . . . Alexander, you make me laugh. You are so innocent, so naïve. Come over here."

"So you deny it, do you? Then what is it, Mother?"

"If you continue to press me on this subject, Alexander, then I will have Erickson throw you out. Let us forget the whole thing and be friends. I am tired of this game, my child. So tired."

"I am tired also, Mother. I want to know the truth."

"You will get nothing out of me."

"I will stop at nothing!" I said, and I meant it.

"You will have to kill me first. I will even provide the gun. Erickson! Get me a gun. My son Alexander wants to kill his mother!"

"Good God, Mother! What harm can come from telling me the truth? Is it that horrible? Don't you know that if you refuse to tell me I will be left with my imagination, which can come up with far worse things, I'm sure!"

"Erickson!" she called. "Erickson will show you out. Erickson, my son is leaving now!"

Erickson came into the room and observed my mother with a look of deep concern.

"Erickson! My son is leaving . . . Erickson, my son is leaving, Erickson, my son is leaving!"

My mother was losing her mind before my eyes. She had lost all sense of reality. In a moment she began to dance around the room and to speak in a singsong voice:

"Erickson, my son is leaving, Erickson, my son is leaving, Erickson my son my son! Is leaving! Erickson my son my son is leaving!"

Erickson stood next to me and watched my mother move around the room, moving her arms about and talking gaily to herself. He turned to me and said: "She has snapped. It has happened before. Watch her and make sure she doesn't hurt herself. I will get the doctor."

I approached her and put my hands on her shoulders to keep her still.

"Alexander, you have ruined me. You will know the truth about your father."

"You will tell me then."

"Yes, I will tell you."

"It was Alvarez, wasn't it?"

"Yes, it was Alvarez."

"Thank you Mother. Thank you very much," I said. "It is better to know the truth."

"It was Alvarez. It was Delvaux. It was Stein. And it was Remick."

Incredible as it may sound I am the child of four gentlemen. The story is as follows: My mother, at the time of her pregnancy, had been the mistress to all four gentlemen. She explains this by saying that she had been in love with each of them, that she preferred no one to another, and that she divided her time equally among them. And they were all aware of the arrangement. She was an extremely popular woman of great beauty and intelligence. Each man considered it his privilege to have her, if only partially.

But on the occasion of her becoming pregnant with me, there was of course a great deal of argument and jealousy over just who the father was, and there was no way of telling. The fact is, I have been told, that none of the men much wanted a child, and each of them would have done anything to get out of the responsibility of fathership.

Thus it was decided, on the suggestion of Alvarez, to determine who would become the father of the child by the following system of chance: Should the child be a girl with blue eyes, she would be the child of Delvaux; should the child be a girl with brown eyes, she would be the child of Stein; should the child be a boy with blue eyes, he would be the child of Alvarez; and should the child be a boy with brown eyes, which is how it happened, he should be the child of Remick. The story that there was any money connected with this affair was simply a rumor.

My mother and Mr. Remick were never married, yet for the sake of the child they set up housekeeping together, but the arrangement was by no means agreeable to either of them, and my mother continued seeing her other beaus.

This is the full truth, unadorned by fancy, as difficult as it may be for the reader to accept it as such. There is no element of fiction in it, and it does me a great deal of good to set it down, at last, on paper.

BLUES FOR A BLACK CAT

BORIS VIAN

Translated from the French by Julia Older

TRANSLATOR'S NOTE. *Boris Vian (1920–59) first started writing poetry in 1939. Poetry, however, comprised just one of Vian's creative talents. He not only completed his studies as an engineer but wrote six novels, eleven short stories, five plays, translated books from several languages, played jazz trumpet professionally, composed, sang, and recorded songs, acted in several films, produced two opera librettos, and was an enthusiastic member of the College Pataphysique, or the College for the Science of Imaginary Solutions, founded in 1948.*

During his entire literary career Vian was subject to continual blasting by Parisian circles and the public for attributing a novel about a black American, J'irai Cracher sur Vos Tombes ("I Shall Spit on Your Graves," *1945) to one Vernon Sullivan, when in fact it was not a translation but his own work. This, in conjunction with a song entitled "The Deserter" ("Le deserteur") had their repercussions.*

When in 1951–52 Vian wrote most of the poems Je Voudrais Pas Crever ("I Would Not Like to Die"), *he had just left his wife Michelle Leglise and two children, was harassed by financial problems, and was not selling his works either under the pseudonym of*

Vernon Sullivan or his own name. He also had been asked to let up on the trumpet, due to a heart ailment which had bothered him since childhood.

In 1954 he married a woman from Zurich, Ursula Kubler. Just prior to an attack he told his second wife that he would not reach the age of forty. Disappointed by the film preview of his first novel and perhaps by the constant battle of his literary career, Boris Vian's heart succumbed to his premonition.—J. O.

I

Peter Gna left the movie with his sister. The fresh night air, scented with lemon, felt good after the stuffy atmosphere of the room, painted in Auvergne blue, of which he felt the effects. There had been a profoundly immoral animated cartoon, and Peter Gna, infuriated, made twirls with his Canadian coat and injured a still untouched old woman. Odors preceded the people on the sidewalks. The street, lighted by street lamps and the lights of the cinemas and cars, curled slightly. Things settled down in the cross streets, and they turned toward the Folies-Bergère. A bar every two houses, two girls in front of each bar.

"A lot of syphilis," grumbled Gna.

"All of them?" asked his sister.

"All," assured Gna. "I see them at the hospital, and sometimes they offer themselves under the pretext they are clean bills."

His sister felt a shiver up her spine.

"What are clean bills?"

"That's when there is no more Wassermann reaction," said Gna. "But it proves nothing."

"Men aren't particular," said his sister.

They turned to the right and immediately to the left, and something miaowed under the sidewalk, so they stopped to see what it was.

II

At the beginning the cat didn't feel like fighting, but every ten minutes the cock emitted a strident crow. The cock belonged to the woman on the first floor. They fattened it to eat at an appropriate time. Jews always eat a cock on a certain date. It gives itself to be eaten, one should say. The cat had enough of the cock. If only it played, but no, always on two feet, to try and be smart.

"Take that," said the cat, and he landed a good kick on its head.

This took place on the sill of the concierge's window. The cock did not like to fight, but his dignity— He let out a loud crow and worked on the sides of the cat with his beak.

"Louse," the cat said, "you take me for a beetle! But you're going to change your mind!"

And bam! A head blow in the breastbone.

"Animal of a cock!" Another blow with his beak on the cat's spine and another in the thick of the loin.

"We'll see!" said the cat.

And he bit its neck, but spit out a mouthful of feathers, and before he could see straight, two hits with the wing and he rolled on the sidewalk. A man passed. He stepped on the cat's tail.

The cat jumped into the air, fell back down into the street, avoided a bicycle that rushed by, and established that the sewer measured a depth of about 1 meter 60, with an angle to 1 meter 20 at the opening, but very narrow and full of rubbish.

III

"It's a cat," said Peter Gna.

It was an improbability that another animal could push perfidy to the point of imitating the cry of a cat, usually called miaowing by onomatopoeia.

"How did he fall there?"

"That louse of a cock," said the cat, "and a subsequent bicycle."

"It's you who started it?" asked Peter Gna's sister.

"No," said the cat. "He provoked me by crowing all the time. He knows I abhor that."

"You shouldn't be angry with him," said Peter Gna. "They're going to cut his neck soon."

"Well done," said the cat with a satisfied derisive laugh.

"It's very bad," said Peter Gna, "for you to rejoice in the misfortune of another."

"No," said the cat, "since I myself am in a tight corner." And he cried bitterly.

"A little more courage," said Peter Gna's sister severely. "You aren't the first cat who has fallen into a sewer."

"But I could care less about the others," grumbled the cat, and added: "You don't want to try and get me out of here?"

"Yes, of course," said Peter Gna's sister. "But if you must start fighting with the cock all over again it's not worth the trouble."

"Oh, I'll leave the cock alone," said the cat in a detached tone. He'd had it.

The cock let out a chortle of joy from inside the upper story. Fortunately, the cat didn't hear.

Peter Gna unwound his scarf and placed himself stomach down in the street.

All this stir had attracted the attention of passers-by, and a group formed around the mouth of the sewer. There was a pedestrian in a fur coat, wearing a pleated rose dress which you could see through its opening. She smelled terrifically good. There were two American soldiers with her, one on each side. You didn't see the left hand of the one on the right, the one on the left either, but he was left-handed. Also, the concierge from the house across the street was there, the maid from the bistro across the street, two pimps in soft hats, another concierge, and an old cat mother.

"It's terrible!" said the whore. "The poor animal, I don't want to look."

She hid her face in her hands. One of the pimps compellingly held her a paper on which they could read: "Dresden reduced to small pieces, at least a hundred and twenty thousand dead."

"Men," said the old cat mother who read the title, "it's nothing. Makes no difference to me. But I can't stand to see an animal suffer."

"An animal!" protested the cat. "Speak for yourself!"

But for the moment, only Peter Gna, his sister, and the Americans understood the cat because he had a strong British accent and the Americans were repelled by it.

"The shit with this limey cat!" said the biggest one. "What about a drink somewhere?"

"Yes, my dearest," said the whore. "They're certainly going to get him out of there."

"I don't think so," said Peter Gna getting up. "My scarf is too short and he can't catch hold of it."

"It's terrible!" moaned a concert of sympathetic voices.

"So shut up," muttered the cat. "Let him think."

"No one has a string?" asked Peter Gna's sister.

They found a string, but from all evidence the cat couldn't cling to it.

"It's not working," said the cat. "It passes through my claws and it's very disagreeable. If I had that louse of a cock, I would cram his nose in this rubbish. It smells disgustingly of rat in this hole."

"Poor little thing," said the maid from across the way. "His miaows are enough to break one's heart. It touches me."

"It touches me more than a baby," remarked the whore. "It's too atrocious. I'm going."

"To hell with that cat," said the second American. "Where can we sip a cognac?"

"You've drunk too much cognac," scolded the girl. "You're terrible too. Come, I don't want to hear that cat."

"Oh!" protested the maid. "You could very well help these men and women."

"I would like to," said the whore who melted into tears.

"If you would shut up, up there," repeated the cat. "And then hurry. I'm catching cold."

A man crossed the street. He was bareheaded, tieless, in espadrilles. He was smoking a cigarette before going to bed.

"What is it, Mrs. Grindstone?" he asked, apparently to the concierge.

"A poor cat that some errand boys must have landed in the sewer," interrupted the cat mother. "These errand boys! All of them should be put in houses of correction until they're twenty-one."

"It's the cocks they should put there," suggested the cat. "The errand boys don't sound off all day under the pretext that perhaps the sun is going to rise."

"I'm going to go up to my place again," said the man. "I have something that is going to be of use in pulling him out of there. Wait a minute."

"I hope it's not a joke," said the cat. "I'm starting to understand why the water never runs out of sewers. It's easy getting in, but the inverse maneuvering is a tiny bit delicate."

"I don't see what we can do," said Peter Gna. "You're very badly located. It's nearly inaccessible."

"I know that very well," said the cat. "If I could, I would get myself out."

Another American approached them. He walked straight ahead. Peter Gna explained the situation to him.

"Can I help you?" said the American.

"Lend me your flashlight, please," said Peter Gna.

"Oh yeah!" said the American and held out his flashlight.

Peter Gna again lay down on his stomach and succeeded in catching sight of a corner of the cat. It exclaimed:

"Send down that thing there. It looks like it works. It's Yankee, huh?"

"Yes," said Peter Gna. "I'm going to hold out my Canadian coat. Try to catch onto it."

He took off his fur-lined coat and let it hang into the sewer, holding it by a sleeve. The people began to understand the cat. They became accustomed to his accent.

"Another small effort," said the cat.

And he jumped to catch onto the garment. They heard the cat, this time a terrible curse. The coat escaped Peter Gna and disappeared into the sewer.

"Is it all right?" asked Peter Gna apprehensively.

"In the holy name of God!" said the cat. "I just bumped my skull on something I hadn't seen. Gee whiz! It's throbbing!"

"And my Canadian coat?" asked Peter.

"I'll give you my pants," said the American, and he started to take off his pants to help the rescue.

Peter Gna's sister stopped him.

"It's impossible with the coat," she said. "Won't be better with your pants."

"Oh yeah!" said the American, who began to rebutton his pants.

"What's he doing?" said the whore. "He's black! Don't let him take down his pants in the street. What a pig!"

Some nondescript individuals continued to congregate in a small group. Under the light of the electric lamp the mouth of the sewer assumed a strange allure. The cat grumbled and the echo of his curses reached the ears of the latecomers, strangely amplified.

"I would really like to recover my Canadian coat," said Peter Gna.

The man in espadrilles elbowed his way to open a passage for himself. He carried a broomstick.

"Ah!" said Peter Gna. "Maybe that's going to work."

But before putting it into the sewer the stick stiffened, and his elbow, formed by the arch, stopped him from getting it in.

"You should look for the sewer grille and loosen it," suggested Peter Gna's sister.

She translated her proposition to the American.

"Oh yeah!" he said.

And immediately he began to look for the grille. He stuck his hand into the rectangular opening, pulled, slid, let go, and knocked himself senseless on the wall of the nearest house.

"Take care of him," Peter Gna ordered two women in the crowd, who picked up the American and took him with them to ascertain the contents of the pockets of his pea jacket. In particular, they found a small bar of Lux and a large bar of O. Henry creamed chocolate. In return, he gave them a good vaginal disease he had contracted from a ravishing blonde met two days earlier at Pigalle.

The man with the stick tapped his head with the palm of his hand and said, "Youracat!" and went home.

"He doesn't care about me," said the cat. "Listen, you up there, if you don't hurry a little, I'm going. I'll be able to find a way out."

"And if it starts to rain," said Peter Gna's sister, "you'll be drowned."

"It will not rain," affirmed the cat.

"Then you will run into some rats."

"Makes no difference."

"Ah well, go," said Peter Gna. "But, you know, there are some bigger than you. And they're disgusting. Moreover, don't piss on my Canadian coat!"

"If they're dirty," said the cat, "it's another story. In any case, the fact is that they stink. No, seriously, manage by yourselves up there. And don't worry about your Canadian. I have my eye on it."

He moved out of hearing distance. The man reappeared. He had a net shopping bag at the end of a long string.

"Marvelous!" said Peter Gna. "He's surely going to be able to hold on."

"What is it?" asked the cat.

"Here," said Peter Gna, throwing it to him.

"Ah! That's better," approved the cat. "Don't pull immediately. I'm taking the coat."

A few seconds later the shopping bag reappeared, the cat comfortably installed inside.

"Finally!" he said, soon disentangled from the net. "As for your Canadian coat, shift for yourself. Find a hook, or something. It was too heavy."

"What a good for nothing!" grunted Peter Gna.

Applause greeted the cat upon his exit from the shopping bag. They passed him from hand to hand.

"What a beautiful cat! Poor thing! He's full of mud."

He smelled awfully bad.

"Dry him off with this," said the whore, holding out her lavender-blue silk scarf.

"It's going to get ruined," said Peter Gna's sister.

"Oh, it doesn't matter," said the whore with a great burst of generosity. "It's not mine."

The cat shook hands all around, and the crowd began to disperse.

"So," said the cat, seeing everyone leaving, "now that I'm out I'm no longer interesting? By the way, where's the cock?"

"Shut up," said Peter Gna. "Come have a drink and don't think about the cock anymore."

The man in espadrilles, Peter Gna, his sister, the whore, and the two Americans stayed with the cat.

"We're going to drink together," said the whore, "in the cat's honor."

"She's not bad," said the cat. "What a figure she has! For the most part, I would sleep with her tonight."

"Calm down," said Peter Gna's sister.

The whore shook her two men. "Come! . . . Drink! . . . Cognac! . . ." she articulated laboriously.

"Yeah! . . . Cognac! . . ." responded the two men, rousing themselves simultaneously.

Peter Gna walked ahead carrying the cat, and the others followed him. A bistro remained open on Richer Street.

"Seven cognacs!" ordered the whore. "It's my round."

"You're a winner!" said the cat with admiration. "A little valerian in mine, waiter!"

The waiter served them, and they all joyfully clinked glasses.

"This poor cat must have caught cold," said the whore. "What if we made him drink some beef bouillon?"

Hearing that, the cat nearly choked and spit his cognac everywhere.

"What do they take me for?" he asked Peter Gna. "I'm a cat, yes or no?"

By the light of the fluorescent bulbs, they now saw the type of cat he was. A terrible large cat, with yellow eyes and a William II mustache. His lacy ears confirmed his total virility, and a large white scar, deplete of hair and coquettishly accentuated by a violet border, crossed his back.

"What's that?" asked the American, touching the place. "Wounded, sir?"

"Yep!" answered the cat. "F.F.I."

He pronounced: Ef Ef Ai like he should.

"Fine," said the other American, vigorously squeezing his paw. "What about another drink?"

"Okey doke!" said the cat. "Got a butt?"

The American extended his cigarette case without malice for the cat's atrocious British accent. The cat thought he would oblige him by pulling out his American slang. The cat chose the longest and lighted it with Peter Gna's lighter. Each took a cigarette.

"Tell us about your wound," said the whore.

Peter Gna found a fishhook in his glass and left soon thereafter to fish out his Canadian coat.

The cat blushed and lowered his head.

"I don't like to talk about myself," he said. "Give me another cognac."

"It's going to make you sick," said Peter Gna's sister.

"No," protested the cat. "I have armored guts. A real cat's gut. And then, after that sewer—Bahh! How it smelled of rat!" He gulped his cognac.

"Holy cow! What a kill!" said the man in espadrilles in admiration.

"The next in a glass of orangeade," specified the cat.

The second American moved away from the group and sat down on the wall bench. He put his head in his hands and started to throw up between his legs.

"It was," said the cat, "in April of '44. I had come from Lyon where I had contacted the cat Lion Plouc, who was also with the Resistance. A cat up to snuff, moreover. Then he was taken by the cat Gestapo and deported to Buchenkatze."

"It's terrible!" said the whore.

"I'm not worried about him. He'll get out of it. So leaving him, I went back up to Paris, and in the train I had the misfortune of meeting a female cat. The trollop! The slut!"

"You must watch your language," Peter Gna's sister reprimanded.

"Excuse me," said the cat, and he took a large gulp of cognac. His eyes lighted up like two lamps and his mustache bristled.

"I passed one of those nights in the train," he said stretching himself with complacence. "Good God! What a kidney attack. Hup!" he concluded, because he had the hiccups.

"So?" asked the whore.

"So, that's it!" said the falsely modest cat.

"But your wound?" asked Peter Gna's sister.

"The feline's patron had hobnailed shoes," said the cat, "and he saw the tail, but he missed it. Hup!"

"That's all?" asked the whore, disappointed.

"You wanted him to cream me, huh?" mocked the cat sarcastically. "Well, you have a ripping mentality, you do! In fact, you never go to the Pax Vobiscum, do you?"

It was a hotel of the district. Briefly, a house of ill repute.

"Yes," answered the whore without evasion.

"I'm a pal of the maid's," said the cat. "Does she knock me around!"

"Ah?" said the whore. "Germaine?"

"Yes," said the cat. "Ger-hup-maine."

He finished his glass in one gulp.

"I would very much like to roll a tricolor," he said.

"A what?" asked the whore.

"A female three-colored cat. Or else a small cat, not too experienced." He laughed disgustingly and winked his right eye. "Or the cock! Hup!"

The cat rose on his four paws, his back arched, his tail stiff, and bristled up his spine.

"Hang it all!" he said. "That bothers me!"

Uneasy, Peter Gna's sister rummaged in her purse.

"You don't know one?" the cat asked the whore. "Your friends are not cats?"

"You're a pig," answered the whore. "Forward ladies and gentlemen."

The guy in espadrilles didn't talk much, but excited by the cat's conversation, he drew near the whore.

"You smell good," he said to her. "What is it?"

"Flowers of Sulfur, by Oldpal," she said.

"And that?" he asked, putting his hand there. "What is that?" He placed himself on the side vacated by the sick American.

"Come on, my dear," said the whore, "be good."

"Waiter!" said the cat. "A crème de menthe!"

"Ah, no!" protested Peter Gna's sister. "Well!" she said, seeing the door open.

Peter returned with his Canadian coat full of refuse.

"Stop him from drinking," she said. "He's completely smashed."

"Wait!" said Peter Gna. "First, I must clean my Canadian coat. Waiter! Two vacuums!"

He hung his Canadian coat on the back of a chair and vacuumed copiously.

"Funny!" said the cat. "Waiter! This crème de menthe, hup! It's you, my Savior!" he exclaimed soon after, clasping Peter Gna. "Come, I'll pay the tab."

"No, my old chap," said Peter Gna. "You're going to catch a cold."

"He saved me!" roared the cat. "He pulled me from a hole full of rats where I would have died."

Moved, the whore let her head fall on the shoulder of the man in espadrilles, who let go of her and went to finish himself off in a corner.

The cat bounded onto the counter and emptied the remaining cognac.

"Brrr!" he said, rapidly shaking his head from right to left. "It goes down hard. Without him," he howled, "I would be finished!"

The whore flopped on the counter, her head in her elbows. The second American left her and stationed himself near his compatriot. Their vomit synchronized, and they designed the American flag on the floor. The second charged himself with the forty-eight stars.

"Into my arms. Hup!" concluded the cat.

The whore dried a tear and said, "But he is kind!"

In order not to vex him, Peter Gna kissed the cat on the forehead. The cat squeezed him between his paws and suddenly let go and collapsed.

"What's the matter with him?" asked Peter Gna's sister apprehensively.

Peter Gna pulled a speculum from his pocket and put it into the cat's ear.

"He's dead," he said after having looked. "The cognac went to his brain." They watched it seep out.

"Oh!" said Peter Gna's sister and began to cry.

"What's the matter with him?" asked the whore uneasily.

"He's dead," repeated Peter Gna.

"Oh," she said, "after all the trouble we went through!"

"He was such a good cat, and he knew how to chat," said the man in espadrilles, who came back.

"Yes!" said Peter Gna's sister.

The waiter from the bistro still hadn't said anything, but he appeared to come out of his torpor.

"That makes eight hundred francs."

"Ah," said Peter Gna, upset.

"It's my turn," said the whore, who took one thousand francs out of her beautiful red leather purse. "Keep the change, waiter."

"Thank you," said the waiter. "What must I do with that?" He pointed to the cat with a look of disgust. A stream of crème de menthe ran over the cat's fur, forming a complicated network.

"Poor little thing," sobbed the whore.

"Don't leave him like that," said Peter Gna's sister. "We must do something."

"He drank like a hole," said Peter Gna. "It's stupid. There's nothing to do."

The noise on par with Niagara, which had been in the background since the Americans left, came to a fresh halt. They got up together and approached the group.

"Cognac!" ordered the first.

"Dodo, my big boy!" said the whore. "Come!" She entwined each in an arm.

"Excuse me, ladies and gentlemen," she said. "I must go put my babies to bed. Poor little cat, all the same—an evening that started out so nicely."

"Good-bye, Madame," said Peter Gna's sister.

The man in espadrilles tapped Peter Gna's shoulder affectionately without saying anything, with an air of condolence. He shook his head, apparently sorry, and left on tiptoe.

Obviously, the waiter was sleepy.

"What are we going to do?" asked Peter Gna and his sister didn't answer.

So Peter Gna put the cat in his fur-lined coat, and they left in the night. The air was cold and the stars exploded one by one. Chopin's funeral march, played by the bells in the churches, made known to the populous that one o'clock in the morning had just sounded. Slowly, they cleared a path through the sharp night.

They arrived at the corner of the street. Black, greedy, the sewer waited at their feet. Peter Gna opened his Canadian coat. He took out the completely stiff cat with care, and his sister caressed it without saying anything. And then, softly with regret, the cat disappeared into the hole. It went: "Glop!" and with a satisfied smile, the mouth again closed.

THE FLIES: SYMPHONIC VARIATIONS FOR STRINGS AND WIND, PERCUSSION AND INSECTICIDES

WILLIAM HEINESEN

Translated from the Danish by Hedin Brøner

TRANSLATOR'S NOTE. *It seems a miracle that the tiny Faroe Isles—isolated by their remote location midway between Iceland and the Shetlands, beaten and buffeted by the gales and surf and tidal races of the North Atlantic, and supporting only a bare forty thousand souls on their barren and rocky shores—have been able to develop a full-blown microcosmic culture, complete with painting, sculpture, music, graphic design, poetry, drama, and fiction. No less miraculous is the fact that despite many centuries of foreign domination, the Faroese people have preserved their own language, which is entirely distinct from Norwegian and Danish but rooted in the same Old Norse mother tongue.*

During the centuries in which other European nations were developing and recording their modern literature, the Faroese language was forced to yield entirely to Danish on the written page, surviving only as a vernacular. This was because Danish had been imposed as the language of education, public administration, law, trade, and religion—a situation persisting well into the present century. It was therefore natural for Faroese writers born about the turn of the century to publish their works in Danish. The younger writers of today have long since turned to Faroese and made it a flourishing literary language.

William Heinesen, the Grand Old Man of Faroese literature, was born in Torshavn in 1900. He began his writing in Danish and has continued to use that language publicly up to the present time despite his fierce patriotism, his jealous concern for Faroese autonomy under the Danish crown, and his energetic support of projects to further develop and strengthen his native tongue. It is ironic that he has become the most versatile and imaginative writer of Danish today, clearly outstripping his mainland cousins in range of style and grandeur of ideas. In his own land he was first known as a painter and lyric poet, and he did not begin to write fiction till the 1930s. Since then he has produced many novels and scores of short stories. His novel Noatun *was translated in Britain under the title* Niels Peter *in 1939 but is unfortunately no longer available. Two other novels, however, exist in recent American translations:* The Lost Musicians *(1971) and* The Kingdom of the Earth *(1974). Translations of some of his stories have appeared in* The American-Scandinavian Review *and in the volume* Faroese Short Stories.

The present story is one of the very few that William Heinesen has not given a Faroese setting, but it is related to the others in its madcap fantasies, its contempt of social and political conventions, and its sweeping perspectives of human existence. Even in his quaint and colorful depiction of rugged Faroese folkways, he has never failed to relate the affairs of his tiny native world to the greater truths of life on the Blue Planet. "What man," he once wrote, "can give a true picture of the place where he was born and raised? Torshavn, to be sure, does not distinguish itself in outward beauty, unusual location, or singular achievements. It is merely a bit of small town between the ocean and the mountain moors. But at the same time this spot is not only the capital of a whole little island realm; it is also, in fact, the very navel of the earth! This is where the sun and the moon first made their appearance. This is where night and day began their existence; and here prevails, even now, that stormy, primeval darkness from which all things arose and splendidly unfolded. From a garret window in the old town of Torshavn you first exchanged glances with the Pleiades and felt the kiss of Eternity upon your brow."

"The Flies," titled "Fluerne" in the original, appeared in William Heinesen's short story collection Kur mod onde Ånder ("Cure Against Evil Spirits"), *published by Gyldendal, Copenhagen, in 1967. It appears here for the first time in English.—W. H.*

Pont-aux-Anes, 11 Sept. 66.

Arrived early today in this forgotten little village behind its seven hills. First impression: bull's eye! Here at last is that blue solitude that I've been dreaming about—azure sky, smokey-blue mountain ridges, and far off on the western horizon, the blue-black ocean. Not that insipid old lake, the Mediterranean, but the proud, open Atlantic.

Quite a large house. One of those southern French farmhouses one remembers from Cezanne's and van Gogh's paintings. "House of the Hanged Man." Crooked and cracked, with sun-scorched tile roof and a curiously inconsistent placement of windows and doors. Owned by a small group of artists. Not much used. The darkish stone steps of the stairway worn hollow by the feet of many generations. Deep cellar without windows, evidently also without flooring. Up above, two rooms practically empty and two sparsely furnished. Small kitchen with sink and cupboards, folding table, bench, two stools. Room with divan, table and chair. Primitive. Cozy. Up here the view is shut off by low, dense treetops.

I chose the small room as my den. The big rooms have more light but don't please me. They have a penetrating smell of decay, and the walls are full of cracks. The chamber with the hidden view—this secret woodpecker's nest in the depths of an unknown forest—just the kind of thing I've had in mind!

Steadied the wobbly table with cardboard pads. Set up the typewriter and the tablet of writing paper. Two thousand sheets of soft, cheap paper—the kind you can really be lavish with.

Filled my pipe and enjoyed my solitude for a while, luxuriating in the absolute isolation. A rapture that sometimes comes upon one quite unexpectedly. A timeless interval of stolen happiness and forgetfulness bordering on the primitive. . . .

And then I come down once more out of the blissful vacuum of timelessness and return to the hour and the present.

A process that does not take place without a certain anguish. Something like birth pains! There is a whirring complaint in your ears, as during the landing of a plane. You throw a pained glance at the smuggler's ware of absolute freedom over there on the customs counter, and then at the ominous signs of double identity in your passport. Nod to your *alter ego* in cold recognition—nod to that immortal antagonist in your heart who is constantly waiting to meet you, saintly and silent, but maliciously watching you in secret triumph from the darker side of your being. . . .

Well. But at least you are once more *here* and in the present. In this world, in this life, whose merciless spotlight stabs into your eyes and whose troublesome and insistent throng of problems flaps about your ears.

Hurrah! I shudder—therefore I *am!*

The only sure thing that I know is this—I intend to concentrate on this work that I was dreaming of and planning in the tumult and restlessness of Paris. "The Sacred Dog"—a *comédie de moeurs.* A kind of serious farce. A comedy in the elevated style. Takes place in an abstract world—half medieval, half modern. Something about a happy couple, the master glass-mosaicist Benedict and his young wife Gloria and their two-year-old daughter Rosvita (the apple of their eye, the hope of their future—life's very meaning!) and about the dog Prosper, which saves the little child from the jaws of the wolf (or some such thing), but which suffers a hero's death and subsequently is idolized by the people as a martyr and a saint. . . .

This, then, is the general outline of the plot—a medieval legend. But parallel to it runs another plot tied to the present time, in which the *audience* keeps interfering with the course of the action, expressing its thirst for sensation mixed with a keen critical sense (at times serious and at others witty), but also with ludicrous narrow-mindedness—all the religious and political intolerance of our time. Police and firemen are unable to prevent this modern audience from intruding on the stage; the medieval characters are charged with blasphemy, communism, and secret collaboration with foreign powers; a herd instinct (only too typical of our time!) gets free reign. They demand that Benedict and Gloria be arrested, little Rosvita placed in a children's home, and the dog Prosper lynched. A tragedy seems inevitable: two incompatible worlds are in sharp confrontation, the encounter seems catastrophic—but then the unexpected happens.

Just what happens isn't clear to me yet, but it will come.

For the time being I am working on the first act.

The *cathedral*, which has been under construction for generations, is nearing completion. Benedict is just about to put the finishing touches on the mosaic pattern of the stained-glass window above the great entrance. Sunlight is streaming through the colored glass. The organist makes his great instrument resound. Life is new and overwhelming, fantastically creative, full of hope. Man's concept of the world is marked by a grand, deeply harmonious simplicity; it is a beautifully limited, meaningful universe within heaven's divine system of spheres. . . . Alas, this *simplicitas* is of course the very thing that I need and long for. Like a vagabond longing for plain bread. Like a thirsty wanderer in the desert longing for clear water.

The fact of the matter is that I am unspeakably weary of the present time, with its shattered image of the universe, with its false ideologies, its blind love of entertainment, its destructive mentality, its constant mortal struggle to find a deeper meaning and sense to everything. Need to find some universal values (sounds sentimental I know!). Not some metaphysical-Archimedian point outside the universe—heaven forbid! No, *that's* not it. A basic human vantage point. Or if nothing else, then at least a temporary sanctuary (if I may be so bold), a refuge from our senseless and catastrophic mania for technology and profit—which, having gained control of the entire globe and ensured its ruin, is well on the way toward conquering and poisoning outer space as well.

Haven't come here merely to enjoy peace and solitude, obviously.

Hardly imagine I'll be able to devote myself unhampered to a frenzy of work either, though (don't dare hope so—naturally hope so anyway!).

Fully realize that I am at the mercy of unpredictable, ambivalent powers—powers that seem hostile and unavoidable.

Not altogether evil ones, perhaps.

I'm secretly clinging to that hope.

There are some insects here. Ants, earwigs. Some disgusting bugs. A host of flies. In the foliage outside an orchestra of cicadas is making ear-splitting music.

Smashed three wasps or hornets, along with some unidentifiable, long, adroit devil with many legs and hooks and antennas. I let a ground beetle hold its ground. Also keep peace with spiders. Would most of all like to keep peace with all living things, naturally. Unrealistic? Naturally. An age-old anchoritic dream. . . .

Hadn't figured on this plague of insects.

This evening some mosquitoes on the wing. I decide to hunt them down mercilessly. My *alter ego,* the nihilist in my heart, who has a certain indelicate taste for destruction, eagerly supports me:

"Of course! After all, what use do we have for all these depraved creatures, these soulless little devils with their ingeniously designed mechanisms of murder and procreation? They comprise four fifths of the animal kingdom. They are some hundreds of millions of years older than we, and the world once belonged to them alone. Will do so again, no doubt. They can afford to wait. We others can't."

Good night.

12th.

Uncomfortable day. Oppressive heat. In spite of good inspiration unable to get started with my writing because of pesty flies and song of the cicadas. Slept badly last night because of the mosquitoes. Some bedbugs here, too—or else some other unappetizing parasite that's bent on sucking blood just like the mosquitoes, producing itches and swellings.

The song of the cicadas is in itself, of course, admirable enough.

One unconsciously paints a picture of this demonic mini-orchestra, these hosts of energetically and senselessly playing male beings, all in apocalyptic attire, with wings and green spectacles (red, come to think of it), all equipped with the same inhuman energy, all feverishly determined to maintain an idiotic musical tradition millions of years old, a soul-consuming machinery of a serenade—or whatever it is.

But as I said there is no denying that it all has a certain elemental strength. Somewhat reminiscent of Schönberg's later orchestral works—the atonal ones. Also makes one think of the endless floods of conformist dance music that stream out through every loudspeaker day and night. That also possesses elements of the jungle and of a remote age. And is produced by monomaniac and infatuated males.

The sensitive flageolet solos of the mosquito are undeniably more personal. Also have a more dramatically challenging relationship to the listener. Romantic opera arias. After all, those cynical little harpies are after nothing less than your heart's blood. Granted that the stilettos and hypodermic needles that they use are cleverly designed—they are nonetheless *malpropre* and have the ability to introduce incurable illnesses into your vital fluids.

There is no mosquito netting to be had in this place, and naturally no chemical insecticide either. Just flypaper. The shopkeeper offered to get me the other things from Anse Espagnole. I bought twelve rolls of flypaper. For the time being have hung six of them under the ceiling in my work- and bedchamber and in the kitchen. They are already woolly with flies. It looks disgusting but seems to be quite effective. Toward evening only a few flies in the bedchamber. But in the empty parlors there is an infernal buzzing of insect wings (also at night, it seems to me). I shut the door to these abominable quarters.

The neighbor's wife, who acts as a sort of caretaker for this house, shakes her head at my flypapers, doesn't understand my abhorrence of flies, claims they are useful. For example maggots of flies are supposed to be a good remedy for eye infections. I asked her in disgust how this is done. Oh, quite simply! The flies lay their eggs in the infected eyes of children, and the maggots eat away all the diseased matter. God has a purpose with all things.

With mosquitoes and bedbugs too? Or what about scorpions?

She nods her head seriously and knowingly. Scorpions wouldn't hurt a fly, and a mosquito bite is nothing to make a fuss about. Anyway, monsieur, there aren't so very many insects here!

She throws me a warm smile—tempting and somewhat teasing. Is quite young. Her olive-tan skin is clear and delicate, her eyes steel gray; very willing and energetic; delightfully awkward in her movements, like a doe or a young heifer. To my surprise, has the same name as the stained-glass artist's wife in my comedy fantasia—*Gloire*.

Well, it's quite possible that I've been taking these insects too seriously.

13th.

Another uncomfortable day after a bad night. Same humid heat. But mosquito netting and various insect powders have arrived.

Sat at my typewriter for several hours without producing more than a few lines. These impudent, annoying flies, always wanting to kiss everything with their snouts! They come in all styles and sizes here—even the greenish stable fly is among them. Comes from the pigsty in the neighbor's courtyard, which also teems with dung beetles, carrion beetles, and all sorts of other queer things.

Forgot to do my marketing. Have nothing but coffee and stale bread in the house. Ate supper at Le Bouton d'Or, the village inn, which is crawling with cockroaches. One of these charming creatures followed me home and hid in the depths of my typewriter, where it was impossible to get at it. No doubt it will turn out to be a pregnant female. Then we'll have still more pleasant guests.

Gloire, the steel-eyed doe with the mocking smile (actually, a medieval Madonna smile—"Gothic"!), helped me hang up a mosquito net, but refuses to participate in the extermination program itself.

14th.

Another unsuccessful day after a restless night. There must be a hole in the mosquito net; at least there was a mosquito inside. A strange new soloist has joined the insect orchestra; it produces a high-pitched, buzzing sound from the wall just over my head.

Possibly a *grillon,* according to Gloire; seems to be some sort of cricket or deathwatch.

The insect spray from Anse Espagnole appears to be quite ineffective. Same holds true for certain white powders, in spite of skulls-and-crossbones and scientific rigmarole on the labels. Gloire can't conceal her triumph. She is obviously on the side of the insects.

Changed the flypapers. At least they are more reliable. But how disgusting! What is it they remind me of? Old doomsday pictures by Memling, Brueghel, Bosch. Modern extermination camps. Open mass graves.

Symbols of destruction.

Set fire to them down in the yard. They burn well. The crematory functions splendidly. Himmler gives a sigh of relief. Eichmann washes his hands. General Ky regards the napalm-ravaged villages of his homeland with satisfaction. . . .

Couldn't collect myself for writing today either.

Oh, well. But my dear "medieval" friends are with me still, in spite of all, and are doing their best to take form. *Gloria* with the sarcastic, enigmatic, and overbearing smile—the delightfully helpful and cheerful one; imagine—she can still be found in the world today, in the flesh, with her passionate tenderness for children and animals and all living things that need a helping hand! This primitive compassion—surely one dares hope that it still is a reality?

Benedict, the honest and skillful craftsman, is still working patiently on his stained-glass window and is making fine progress day by day despite rather poor technical equipment—has a sense of pride—feels a compulsion to produce a respectable piece of work. No cheating here. In his day and age bargains, mass production, assembly-line slavery, and consumer mentality were unknown. Also big industries (those impersonal, insectlike tyrants of our time, with their monstrous appetite and their ubiquity!). Those times were not in any way like ours—near-perfect where the technical-mercantile is concerned but barbarously backward in human relations. Base thirst for profit had not yet become the driving force in society's machinery and the cause of war between peoples. Warfare was still a matter of individual heroism and not of impersonal insecticides aimed from above against defenseless women and children. Magnanimity was still a living reality. Those were times when people were high-minded enough to accept even dumb animals into their great, universal brotherhood—when a Francis of Assisi could communicate with the birds, and when even a dog could achieve the dignity of a saint!

At this point my *alter ego* breaks into a Mephistofelian smile. A bedtime story for children? Well, call it whatever you like. Your own day and age is naturally too barbaric to be able to regard it with anything but scorn. But people at that time did not sneer at the thought of this sacred dog—did not regard the "stupidity" of it with malicious satisfaction. They smiled. It amused them. It elicited a sublime kind of humor—something that our cynical and restless race has lost completely. Nowadays we can afford to smile only in a superior and macabre way, sardonically, without hope—but with sophistication and existentialistic nausea. . . .

I throw my antagonist a sideward glance. Still this demonic sneer in his conceited face! It's getting on my nerves. Is that fashion snob going to come and ruin my good intentions with his stuffy-nosed *desespoir?* I make use of my authority as a superego and force him out. Wipe him out. He disappears with a puff.

Not altogether, of course. But some time usually goes by before he gets a chance to re-establish himself, and then I'm left in peace for a while.

Went for a long walk this afternoon. The same blue *limpidezza,* the same grandiose view. The ocean in the distance. To the south, the snow-clad double mountain peak with the rich name *La Maman.* Climbed up into a low pine at the edge of a cliff; sat there watching the sun set and Sirius rising from the sea, spectrally twinkling. Felt the immense, primitive pleasure of sitting in a tree.

Thought to myself: Life is a mystery, overwhelmingly bright and wonderful, overwhelmingly dark and cruel—inconceivable and incomprehensible. Of all living things, man is the only one that ventures to try to analyze and test its laws and patterns. In the phenomenal drama of life we, in contrast to all other creatures, are both actors and spectators. Truly remarkable! We see the stars twinkling and know that these are phenomena quite beyond our own dimensions, but at the same time we know that they are the product of our own eyes, and that the light they send forth is a reflection of a light within us.

As I sat here after that lovely evening walk, trying to put the above thoughts on paper, I suddenly felt a little sting in my back below the shoulder blades, followed by an insufferable smarting. A wasp? Perhaps a scorpion? The devil that had stung me was apparently still there; I could feel it wriggling and moving about inside my clothes. You're not going to get away with it alive, I thought, jumping up. I carefully took off my shirt in hopes of finding the aggressor unharmed, and I succeeded. He was sitting inside my shirt, a little red fellow no larger than a flea, but it *was* no flea—more like a tiny spider or a large tick. Shiny vermilion.

I scooped the little vermin into an empty matchbox. Maybe Gloire could tell me what the wretched thing was. But when I went to look at him again later, he was gone.

15th.

Felt that infernal insect bite all night long. It did its part in ruining my sleep. In addition there were the usual mosquitoes and bugs—and then *le grillon*.

Asked Gloire this morning whether she knew anything about that little red devil with the shameless bite. She smiled and asked me to show her my back.

"It's just a common ordinary flea bite!" she said, laughing the way strong women laugh at hypochondriac men—somewhat maliciously and yet with a bit of tenderness underneath. Whereupon we react by taking offense, which we well know is ridiculous; but after all, we masters of creation don't want to be the women's pets!

The new flypapers are already full of flies and mosquitoes, dead and half dead. Some of the half-dead ones give off faint singing sounds. In a minor key. Insects always express themselves in a minor key. The busy bee, the carefree fly—indeed, even the bumble bee, which seems so contented—they are all tuned in a minor key.

From one of the flypapers comes a sound like the crying of an infant. The faint, inconsolable voice fills me with disgust. High time to set about changing these unappetizing glue traps, I guess. I take them down from the ceiling, filled with revulsion. Of course I can't avoid looking at them—battlefields of teeming heads and legs, a lot of damned souls squirming in their hell of glue. There is a butterfly among them, too. Think it's the so-called "scarce copper." Too bad. It isn't dead. Its legs are helplessly stuck to that brown syrup; its beautiful flame-red wings are still free and fluttering helplessly. A symbol of destruction. For a moment I drift into a vague feeling of remorse. This flypaper is getting on my nerves.

At noon I had quite a disgusting experience in the kitchen as I stood frying a steak with onions. Something that was lying on the window sill and that looked like a small, withered leaf with a short stem at its base suddenly got up and turned out to be alive, moved forward, flung out a long pincer, and—snap!—a fly sat wedged in the trap. The little monster promptly set about consuming the fly, but when a larger fly showed up nearby it dropped its first victim and snapped up the new one with its scissor. The first one wasn't quite dead yet. The new one was greedily devoured in no time at all. All but the wings. Blood and entrails were still stuck to the inner edge of the scissor. I've rarely seen anything so unappetizing, and I could hardly get my steak down.

I managed to catch the scissor-murderer in an empty matchbox. Will ask Gloire what sort of gangster it is.

17th.

Toward evening yesterday I felt sluggish. Think I had a bit of fever, and the pains from the mysterious insect bite had spread to my neck and the back of my head.

I drank a couple of glasses of *vin cuit* and lay down on the divan.

The drink did me some good. It is mild and rich, with a slight taste of bitter almonds. A local home-brew which I suspect the grocer makes himself. The bottle has a white label with an unreadable inscription. Απαγε Σατανας, is the way I make it out—*Apage Satanas,* "Get thee behind me, Satan!" Sounds ambiguous enough, doesn't it? Underneath this ominous inscription three stars or pentagrams and an unreadable vintage year.

Drank another glass, remembering the old rule of conduct: All good things are three.

Drifted for a moment into contemplation of the inexhaustible magic effect of the figure *three* on—man's mind. The age-old magic of the Trinity. Three Fates. Three Graces. The three ancestors of the races of the earth. The three patriarchs of the Bible. The three brothers of the Norwegian folk tales. The three cardinal virtues. Further: God, King and Country. *Mene tekel upharsin.*

A light rain had begun to fall. The song of the cicadas had died away, but the *grillon* now had company. There were three of them now. They were signaling each other from separate walls. Love signals probably. Three males, each trying to get its own female. Or maybe the same female. And now they were having their wedding in the old brown paneling. The two lovers were no doubt brown and woodlike, too, with great heads heavy with chitin.

Oh, well, best wishes, I thought—and good luck with the mechanics of it!

I enjoyed a couple of drinks in the evening and slept tolerably well for a change. Had a very unpleasant dream toward morning, however.

It was about the little scissor-murderer in the matchbox out in the kitchen. It had broken out of the box, had grown to the size of a lobster, came to take revenge on me for its captivity. I stamped it to death with the heel of my shoe, heard its chitin case crack to pieces with a grinding sound mixed with a bit of dry weeping. Then I set fire to its earthly remains. They burned very well and went up in smoke and nothingness, but afterward I began to have some doubts as to whether it really was an insect that I had murdered and not some kind of human being. That *weeping* was certainly human, at least. Then I changed my form in a strange way. My hands were full of gray warts and had short, bitten-off nails. They weren't my hands! And on my feet I had long military boots. . . .

I woke up with a piping sound in my ear. It wasn't mosquitoes—not crickets either. There were several wind instruments, a little orchestra—most strange, a little flute concerto in ultramodern style. It came from one of the empty parlors. I also seemed to hear a fluttering of wings. Birds? Bats?

It was still night. I was very thirsty, took a large drink of *vin cuit,* went to bed again. The piping concert continued. I was actually enjoying it.

Showed Gloire my captive in the matchbox this morning. It was dead.

"Ah—a *prie-Dieu!*" she said. A pray-to-God. A sacred animal. Had I killed it?

I had caught it alive in this box, I said.

Well but then I had killed it. She gave me a pitying look. A *prie-Dieu* is a virtuous being. To kill it means bad luck. It is absolutely the only animal apart from the lamb and the dove that prays to God. And then the ladybird, of course. Hadn't I seen it praying?

"It caught and killed two flies with its scissor as I watched it," I said.

Yes but what is it we humans do? Don't we kill lambs as well as sheep, and eat them? And even kill each other? And yet pray to God?

I had no answer for her.

"But it isn't dead at all!" she gleefully exclaimed, grabbing me by the arm.

No, the creature was not at all dead—had merely been sleeping or feigning death, and now it unfolded a couple of innocently green wings and took off from the box. Gloire opened the window and shooed the asinine thing out with a kissing sound. Then she turned to me, looked affectionately into my eyes and said, "That meant *luck,* monsieur!"

It sounded suggestively comforting and encouraging.

I told her about the flute concert of the previous night. Yes, it must have been bats, she thought. So one of the windows must not have been shut tight enough. She would go and see.

She disappeared into the buzz of the empty rooms, humming to herself as she went. I heard her laughing in there and talking affectionately, with pursed lips, the way women talk to little children. A while later she returned with a ladybird on the back of her hand. The tiny red toy with black spots on its shell sat still as if it were rapturously listening to her voice. She opened the window again and said something like: "Fly away then, little angel! I know where you want to go! Give my greeting to Our Beloved Little Mother! *Adieu et bonne heure!*"

The ladybird swung aside its wing covers, exposing the watery-clear wings, and disappeared into the blue. I thought to myself: "The little darling will certainly get caught and be eaten up by some insatiable pray-to-God—just wait and see!"

Yes, those were bats that I had heard squeaking all right, said Gloire. There were seven of them hanging under the ceiling in there. Did it matter?

"Let them hang, in God's name," I said. "May their number increase!"

18th.

Took the train to Anse this morning, a trip taking a little under an hour. Here in Pont there is no physician. That insect bite on my back, whatever it may be, is still giving me trouble, filling me with disgust, keeping me awake at night, preventing me from concentrating on my work.

The physician's waiting room was crowded. A peculiar old man entertained me with stories about his complicated case. To tell the truth, I understood hardly anything of what he confided, but I nodded in a friendly way in order not to disappoint him. He asked me what was wrong with me. Aha, that was a *mitavenin,* he asserted. They are sometimes dangerous when their poison gets in the blood. It can cause fever and hallucinations. Some go mad from it.

Mad?

"Yes, quite mad. I had a cousin. . . ."

But now it's his turn to go in to the doctor, and he doesn't have time to tell me about his hapless cousin.

Mitavenin. I sit there ruminating on this peculiar name and drift into feverish etymological speculations.

Poisonous tick?

The doctor is a striking-looking elderly man with large gray mustaches á la Marechal Petain—a blacksmith-type man that is quite common down here. He looks as if he had eaten his fill of iron.

"That thing?" he says, jabbing his finger at my back. "That's a flea bite."

I protest weakly, but of course I have to bow to professional judgment.

"What is a *mitavenin?*" I ask as I am dressing.

Mitavenin? He doesn't know the word, hasn't heard it before. Where have I run across it? Oh, from *him*—Monsieur Metterin, the barber? Metterin is crazy.

That's that. I pay and leave.

At the pharmacy they wonder at my dissatisfaction with the insecticides they had sent through the grocer in Pont. But if I want something more drastic they can get it from Bayonne. It's a kind of anaesthetizing poison gas, *Lamortsansphrase,** containing a chitin-dissolving chemical. This miracle remedy can be sent direct to me from Bayonne along with an automatic compressed-air syringe operated by an electric battery.

The pharmacist hands me an illustrated brochure.

I'll think it over.

In reality there shouldn't be so much to think over. My situation has become so acute that a decision has to be made. The decision to go all out in the battle against this insect plague, or to retreat from the field. I am of course free to pack up my few belongings, break camp, move on and find another and supposedly better refuge.

Why the devil don't I decide to move on, then? What is it that's tying me to this delapidated and filthy nest in Pont, in spite of everything? Common sense tells me to leave it as soon as possible. It was all a mistake. Fine, so go ahead and correct it then!

But for some hitherto unexplained reason I still don't feel like heeding this voice of reason. My *alter ego,* the irrationalist in my heart, rejects the convenient and, as he calls it, the cowardly alternative of flight. Wants me to "play out the entire line," whatever *that* is supposed to signify. There is a secret, pleasurable curiosity involved, too, I must confess. Devil take it anyway.

It's this *Gloire,* of course.

I see her with hallucinatory clearness as she stands lost in thought, gazing into the blue yonder after sending her message to the Holy Mother via the ladybird. Charmingly awkward, a bit childish—like one of Degas' ballet dancers when they forget themselves and relax in a noncommittal position of rest.

No, I couldn't make up my mind. Felt a bit exhausted for the time being. Had to have time to weigh the whole matter thoroughly. Took myself a drink and stretched out on the divan. Far from being in good form. Felt humiliated and miserable. Had a

* Lamortsansphrase is also the name of a general in Heinesen's surrealistic poem "Jam Session 1959."—W.H.

headache and ringing in my ears. And a painful, increasing swelling on the under side of my left wrist—wasp sting probably—maybe scorpion. Think at any rate that I've seen two peculiar, sneaky types with pale faces and twisted tails disappearing into a crack in the kitchen floor.

From the woolly flypaper those hair-fine songs of complaint continued to sound forth—those faint death rattles. There was a blue dragonfly stuck to one of them. It looked like a ballerina in distress. Some injustice has been done her. She's been delivered over to humiliation and destruction. She's at Death's door, is doubled over in an ungainly posture. It is terrible to witness. An evil fate has struck her; she is in the grip of that terrible glue. A Belsen prisoner.

You can at least stop lying there and looking at it, I tell myself irritably.

It seems that you cannot, smugly remarks my *alter ego*. He is feeling talkative, I notice, and is cynically taking advantage of my weak condition. I hear him riding his usual hobby horse, the one about "the deep-rooted and never-changing depravity of human nature"—the well-known refrain of all one-eyed misanthropes.

"Just don't put on any airs, old boy," he says with his ostentatious flippancy. "Everything that is sensational is pleasurable. Even that which strikes terror. In all candor now: don't you always feel a certain *convoitise* when you read about rape or murder in the newspapers? Or about lightning—earthquakes—floods—danger of war? Or when you secretly enjoy looking at one of Brueghel's or Goya's visions of horror? Or shudderingly enjoy the merciless violence in Michelangelo's picture of Doomsday? Or the petrified, visible death cry in Picasso's Guernica? Or what about Dante's Inferno or the structured terror of the Greek tragedies?"

I try to collect myself and contradict all this ignorant talk. (After all, doesn't the sight of misery and need goad the normal spectator to protest—perhaps to active help? And then there is such a thing as *catharsis*, too! Doesn't that blockhead know that?) But I give it up. Through the buzzing of the flies and the chirping of the cicadas I can hear him continue his smug harangue about the absurdity of life, the human heart's elemental cruelty and lust for destruction, which is exceeded only by our insatiable curiosity—and about the euphorizing extract, the dark sweetness that art with its demonic power manages to draw from suffering and ugliness.

The modern world image—yes indeed. The ingenious *homo*

sapiens of Victorian times, the glorious conquerer, Nietzsche's *Übermensch*—exposed as an incorrigible beast of prey, a pray-to-God, whose nature expresses itself through greed, lust for power, cowardice, algolagnia, hypocrisy!

—Defense against *whom?* It's *yourself*, my dear sir. Actually, there is no defense—none necessary either, for our highly perfected monster has, among other things, arranged for his own exit from the scene! Is merely waiting for someone to come and press the button and put an end to the whole questionable tragicomedy.

Only too true, I must admit. But only half the truth. The dark one. But the other half! That's the one that I . . . ! No, I'm too tired to go over it again now.

The Sacred Dog? My antagonist could hardly conceal a malicious smile.

I got up from the divan with some difficulty. Got another drink from the kitchen. Felt quite forsaken and unwanted for a moment. Was I on the point of capitulating to the hated defeatist in my heart?

I stood in front of the kitchen mirror and looked him searchingly in the eye. Yes, we resembled each other closely enough, with obvious features of our common apelike ancestor, the only beast of prey among the primates—the fellow with the bloody club, and with the bushy hair and beard that I've acquired lately. He sent me a long, dogged, care-worn look, old as the universe. Our eyes met in pain and hatred, and in our hideous, fleshy ears there sounded that agonized sigh which runs through all creation. . . .

Took another drink. By and by got on a reasonably even keel and in the right mood. Sat down at the typewriter. And here I still sit, having once more scribbled an ungodly amount! Guess it wasn't exactly what I had meant to fill my many clean sheets with, but what the devil, now I simply can't bring this miserable reporting to an end! A useless occupation, perhaps—but at least it bucks me up, rids me of that infernal maelstrom whose cruel dimples threaten to suck me under in the course of these wretched days.

20th.

Had a strange dream last night. It is still very vivid in my mind. I hasten to record it:

. . . Hung in some indeterminate place between heaven and

earth. Pitch-dark night. All alone—like a child in its mother's womb or a cosmonaut in space. Felt a moment of agony—but only a moment, and then I let go and fell down from the ceiling, where I had been hanging by my toes. I felt the air pressure against the webs between my huge, spread-out fingers. The blood pulsed strongly through my veins. I listened with enormous, cocked ears. Life returned triumphantly to my heart. The darkness was filled with a dissonant, stirring music. The morning of life was dawning anew, with hunger and sexuality, jubilant anticipation and devil-may-care courage.

I sailed slowly and on great, silent wings through a warm semi-darkness full of comestibles—flying hash, literally speaking, alive and fragrant with spices. I ate greedily and eagerly and exposed my pointed teeth in a wide leer. A being of my own kind, but of the opposite sex, passed close by me; teats and lips brushed across my cheek, a little subdued laugh came through her nostrils—provokingly, with a strong smell of skin and hair. Violent electric shocks put my reproductive organs on the alert. But then, unexpectedly: a sharp bite at one of my ears—the cruel warning of a rival! Truly, I was among my own kind—mammals and carnivores with their familiar, age-old individualistic greed, passion and jealousy, battles and copulations, serenades and war cries!

Another bite. The excited breath of the attacker in my ear, a glimpse of his twisted features in the twilight—and then it was a matter of defending oneself as best one could from this aggressor. I bit back. A bloody fight developed at close quarters. We did our best to rip up each other's webs, ears, and genitals with the bayonets of our teeth, to tear each other's eyes out, destroy each other's radar equipment and infra-ultra-piezoelectric apparatus. We clung to each other in desperation, so that the umbrella frames of our wings clinched; we tried to bite into each other's throats, insanely growling and squealing.

I notice to my chagrin that my enemy is my superior. I am deathly wounded, have no more strength, catch a baleful glimpse of my inner archenemy's familiar face with its terrorist leer. My broken fingers ache, my webs shrink up like a chilled scrotum, I fall to earth with a thud, vanquished, blubbering miserably, my hide drenched with blood. But not quite dead yet, for I can still see with one eye and am shudderingly conscious of existing, albeit only as a sad ruin of myself.

To my surprise I find that I am suddenly surrounded by a bevy of old ladies dressed in black—like a pilot who has crashed through the roof of a boardinghouse. An unpleasant smell of pressed flowers; yellowing poetry books; lavender; candlewax; warm, leather-bound hymnbooks; salty tears. All of it curiously old-fashioned, with memories of a bygone, frightfully romantic period of umbrellas and chamber pots. A hoarse gramophone sings out "Jim and I were friends forever." Gently fondling hands and fingertips, bad breath, sentimental cuddling, the bathing of a corpse—what is all this?

Ah, I understand. I am a dead bat that is being examined by carrion beetles. Pensive and solemn gravediggers, undertakers, and black priests crawl around in my horrid, miscarried face with its harelip and blood-smeared snout. Fragments of a professionally comforting and sniveling funeral sermon remain in my ear, the membranes of which are still taut: "The reality of the world is a dwindling life between God and existence." There is also a fading echo of funeral hymns. "*Ach, Mensch, gieb acht!*" "Quoth the raven, Nevermore." And something about

Our circle has no ending;
Lo, all things rise again!

How comforting! The ubiquitous flies are naturally on hand here, too—the blowfly with its spew and excrements—other flies—all busily blowing their noses and wiping their eyes—a few well-dressed, armed flies of finer extraction—elegant predatory flies in uniform complete with decorations—a colorful funeral procession with busy antennae, probosces, and black umbrellas. Rearmost in the procession bugs and earwigs, woodlice and *grillons*—and our friend pray-to-God with its bigoted eyes turned heavenward and its scissor well concealed underneath a costume designed for the purpose.

Here I lie, defenseless and crowned with thorns. . . .

Crowned with thorns?

I wake up with a jerk and struggle free of the itching crown of thorns. —Why, it isn't anything but one of the crowded flypapers, which has fallen from the ceiling and is lying across my forehead! I toss it aside, get stinking glue and fragments of flies on my fingers, have my face all besmeared as well, sit up in agony with a dryness of the throat and throbbing temples.

It is late morning. I reach for the glass with a shaky hand, gradually get back to my old self again, scowl forlornly at the singing of

Zarathustra's Midnight Chorale by all these carrion-diggers. Take another drink. Decide to pull myself together and phone the pharmacy in Anse to order that gas machine or infernal machine that they offered me. It's high time. Thumb excitedly through the brochure. *Lamortsansphrase* (English, Kill Quick; German, *Schnelltöter*). Contains Dichlordiphenyltrichloromethylmethane and Pentachloriddiphenylethane (these interesting millipede words sound promising, I think!). Manufactured by an international cartel, a worldwide business which, on a higher plane, produces chemical and bacteriological agents of eradication for military use in international conflicts and for the furtherance of general genocidal goals.

What more could one possibly demand?

At the local grocer's, where I have been using the telephone, I make an extravagant purchase—thirty new flypapers! I can tell by looking at him (and even more at his wife) that I am suspected of not having all my buttons. The little store is full of wasps, but it doesn't bother them, say the couple in the store—they are immune to insect stings. The wife—she introduces herself as Madame Frelon—is a thin little woman with a piercing look behind her spectacles. She has something on her mind, wishes to talk to me privately, as there are other customers in the store. She takes me into a small back room containing a desk and some files. On the wall a dusty old photo of President Laval.

Madame Frelon speaks a local dialect that is not easy to understand, but I gather that it all concerns the good Gloire.

She visits me now and then, does she not?

Yes, she is responsible for the house. Does various small favors for me.

Madame Frelon looks penetratingly into my eyes and silently shakes her head. Gloire is definitely not responsible for the house. She is a lying hussy whom I should be very cautious of. She is also inclined to steal (Mrs. Frelon crooks her fingers on both hands and makes them crawl in the air like an insect), has been caught lifting things here in the store several times. She is *impudique!*

She is what?

Madame Frelon makes an embracing motion at me and wriggles her hips. Gloire is such a one. Her husband has left her this very morning, couldn't put up with her affairs any longer. She opened his letters and stole things from his stamp collection.

Did I now understand what sort of person she is? Watch your monies, Monsieur; if you have any, keep them on your person always, or deposit them here with us. Don't fall for that cow! *Now you have been warned!*

I thanked her despondently for the information. Madame Frelon showed her hard gums in a tight-lipped smile. I went off with my new flypaper and two bottles of Apage Satanas.

Gloire—a thieving hussy? There must be something wrong with my judgment of people then.

I feel sorry for Gloire. I have long regarded her with admiration. Now I feel a certain tenderness for her as well.

Poor child!

When I got back she was standing in the kitchen, wiping off the table and airing the place out. On the window sill a large bouquet of wild roses that she had brought. She looked refreshed and cheerful, and had a mischievous and very girlish expression in her gray eyes.

"You look so happy today, Gloire," I said. "Has something especially nice happened?"

"On the contrary!" she said with a broad smile. "My husband left me this morning!"

For always?

No. Gloire smiled still more broadly, exposing a gap on the left side of her otherwise perfect row of teeth. Her husband, the rural postman Jose, had been promoted to city postman in Bayonne. Eventually she, too, would leave peaceful Pont and live in the big, restless city by the sea.

She shuddered as if the thought chilled her.

"Don't you have any children, Gloire?"

"Unfortunately not, Monsieur. We have been married for two years. Actually, it is *his* fault. He is so lifeless about it."

She blushed slightly.

"Excuse me, Monsieur—perhaps I should not have said that. But the thing is that he is a stamp collector. He has a large collection. He does not think about anything else."

Suddenly she looked up at me tenderly.

"Monsieur does not look well," she said. "Perhaps he does not get the proper food? Shall I fry for Monsieur a very fine cutlet? Or prepare a ragout? What do you like the best? Something with vegetables!"

I gave her money for meat and vegetables and a couple of bottles of wine.

Felt dull, had a bad headache and ringing in the ears.

The Maelstrom. Charybdis, that terrible drawing thing, was clearly sucking with all its might.

I took a large drink and noticed with a kind of dark elation (like the one you feel in a devilishly designed roller coaster) how I really was heading for the relentless currents where a rudder no longer serves any purpose. Hey, hey!

And just see now: From the foaming breakers out there rises the high cliff where Scylla lives. You can hear her loud, frenetic howling—the same one that broke your sleep when you were a child!

> Mind thee, she hath a dozen dangling feet,
> And six long necks, and on each neck a head
> Most hideous, with a triple row of teeth
> Set close and thick, and reeking of black death.*

Twelve evil shark's eyes glare at me; a gigantic swab of flesh-colored octopus arms whips the sea into a froth. She is not in a joking mood and cannot be induced to smile.

And yet, at last—this slight puckering of the lips on her sixth mouth . . . ?

Skoal, old girl!

I raise my glass with a shaky hand.

Suddenly all the heads are smiling! Just imagine!

Then there is still hope?

Intermezzo.

A loud clanking of sabers and grinding of chitin. A uniformed individual with granulous gray spectacles on its insect face unfurls a pair of large, veined wings and salutes smartly. I notice that he has the emblem of the world insect organization WIO on his cap.

Was I the one who had ordered a doomsday machine from Usaurus, Ltd.? He had come to put some questions to me concerning this matter. He took a seat at the table and brought out his notebook.

Name and address, date of birth, color of hair and eyes, etc.

Identifying marks? Screams in his sleep. Many thanks.

Was I aware of the fact that my maniacal and unchivalrous persecution of innocent representatives of other species and other

* This quotation is from Book XII of *The Odyssey of Homer*, Sir William Harris, trans., London, Oxford University Press, 1925, p. 207.—W.H.

mentalities is not only morally improper but also punishable by law?

Ha, ha! Could this by any chance be *him*—my diabolical symbiont—once again busy with his jokes?

He continues, unaffected by my effort at a superior smile, and with the dry voice of a schoolmaster: Did I not know that insects constitute an indispensable stage in nature's great cycle, partly by destroying and utilizing large quantities of unclean waste matter with which death and digestive processes (particularly caused by my own kind) burden the earth—and partly by their untiring and self-sacrificing service of pollination, without which all life would wilt away, practically speaking?

Further: Could I disprove that many insects are hyperintelligent, that ants and bees, for example, have their own sign language—the bees even a veritable sound language; and that the miserable mammal that calls itself *homo sapiens,* compared with these ingenious winged creatures with their highly developed sense of social organization, can be considered nothing more than a coarse and slothful beast of prey?

I have no answer for this. Weakly object that after all, it isn't *all* insect life that I am after, that this is a matter of simple and necessary measures against harmful pests that happen to be present.

Precisely the same arguments the Nazis used when they pulverized Poland or the Americans when they wiped out Hiroshima and Nagasaki.

This was the limit! I stretched out my arm and exposed the scorpion sting underneath the wrist. I pulled up my trousers and showed him the ravaged moon landscape on my legs and behind my knees.

"That is only the beginning!" he said, breaking into an ominous buzzing. He unfurled his big, clear wings. Nearly looked beautiful for a moment—spotless, angelically free from sin, a sublime personage, a benefactor of all life, exterminator of all evil, lover and collaborator of fragrant flowers.

And here I lay, a conceited ape with a jungle beard and a badly deteriorated soul.

New intermezzo.

From the kitchen emanates an evil smell as of burnt rubber. It is

Gloire cooking supper. Insects and still more insects. *Paté de woodlouse*. Cricket shank with fly-egg-mayonnaise, black-ant caviar, red cicada salad. There will be several of us at the table. Besides Gloire and myself—and my other self, who now has assumed the amusing cover name Monsieur Mitavenin—there will be several prominent representatives of the insect world's industry, cultural life and armed forces, all in full human size. Among the prominent guests is the world renowned physician, Professor Schmarotzenwespe, known for his epoch-making experiments with butterfly larvae in Maidenek and Auschwitz. From the unoccupied parlors, where a simpler meal is being served for the common insect folk, there comes the familiar sound of an animated party, many busy voices at one time, cascades of laughter, self-satisfied courtroom opinions, lesser arguments, applause, flirting, efforts at wanton song, cries of greeting. And then this incessant accompaniment of crackling and creaking chitin. . . .

Professor Schmarotzenwespe, who is my table partner, shows me a tiny hypodermic needle with a fine, nearly invisible point. Interesting, is it not? His lorgnette gleams contentedly.

"Let me show you! Give me your right hand!"

I ward him off. No, not now, Herr Professor, not here . . . !

I feel a hair-fine pain as from a morphine needle—a feeling of thickness in my wrist—wake up with a start.

Afternoon. Buzzing of flies. Singing of cicadas. Gloire has not yet returned—

Felt miserable. Staggered down the stairs, threw up in the yard. The rejected stomach contents were immediately subjected to busy and expert examination by insects rushing in from all directions.

Felt better after my *vomitus*. Hungry and thirsty. Hastily drained a couple of glasses. When was that woman going to come back, anyway? Surely she hadn't skipped off with the miserable twenty francs I entrusted her with? That would be the lowest . . . !

Ah—now I hear her light tread on the stairs. Thank God. Then perhaps all hope is not gone.

21st. Afternoon.

Woke up this morning with a phenomenal headache, but a couple of glasses of the mild and mellow *vin cuit* did wonders.

Am sitting here again, in a relatively good and optimistic mood, determined to bear my vicissitudes calmly.

I am writing this by hand because my typewriter is gone. Gone also is the wallet containing about twenty thousand francs that I had in the breast pocket of my jacket. And my suitcase and a pair of new shoes have disappeared as well.

God knows what she wanted with those men's shoes!

She herself has disappeared, too, and I suppose will never return—for good reasons.

Forgiven. I don't begrudge her the money, the typewriter, the suitcase, or the shoes. Though that thing about the shoes does annoy me a bit.

Never mind.

Will continue this chronicle.

Believe me we had a wild night, Gloire and I—not to forget Monsieur Metavenin, who is trying more and more to tear himself away from our painful companionship, though it naturally gives him some trouble. In dreams this is easy enough—after all it was he, in the shape of a hostile bat, who bit me half to death, and understandably enough it was he who appeared as the well-spoken envoy of the world insect organization WIO. Last night he acted the part of some sort of long-haired Beatle with an insinuating singing voice (though of course well strewn with mosquito bites and bedbug welts on his neck and arms and face!), and had assumed a quite overbearing and presumptuous demeanor toward Gloire—a manner that I cannot abide. I gave him to understand that in the form he had assumed here, he represented a stage in my development that could gain nothing but my contempt at my present level. In the course of an otherwise successful evening meal he abandoned himself, as one might expect (dead drunk as he naturally became!), to a depraved flirtation with the good Gloire. He not only tickled her under the chin, but he also bit her ear lobes and her hair and sucked her eyelids till they grew red and swollen. But when he became presumptuous enough to try to expose her breasts I interfered, and we had a bitter exchange of remarks. When physical violence seemed imminent and Gloire threatened to leave the party, I mobilized my superego with every effort in me, and expelled him from the scene. It was a close shave, and I was just about to lose, but the long and the short of it was that he retreated, humiliated, gnashing his teeth and with hatred in his eyes.

"It almost seems a shame," said Gloire.

"We'll drink to him!" I said, passing it all off. "He is a coarse porno-baboon. One of those exponents of our vulgarizing times, which drag all values down into the muck in cheap sales—even Eros. I am ashamed of him."

"Oh, well—*was* it really so bad?" said Gloire, suddenly pulling up her black sweater so that both her young, high breasts were exposed. A disgusting cockroach ran quickly across one of them. I flicked it away, but then immediately there were more of them, and now it was all I could do to keep her beautiful and maidenly bosom free of these insolent vermin. I flicked and blew, and she giggled ticklishly, with ants on her lips and a gray bug under one eye.

"Come on!" she said with a faint smile.

"Come—what was that?" asked my amazed superego feverishly.

She burst into a loud laugh that went to my very marrow. Her almost naked torso had the hue of dewy grape clusters. Rarely have I seen anything so admirable.

But now there was a sudden change in our relative sizes, as she swelled with increasing speed to the dimensions of an elephant while I shrank correspondingly to the modest size of an insect. In my great confusion at this bizarre state of things I sought refuge in her ear and found myself in a long tunnel dimly glowing with a reddish light and lined with a fine dark fur. Across the end of this tunnel there was a double sliding door. The two halves glided silently apart, opening to an engine room of the kind one sees in modern power stations—neat and clean, without a speck of dust on the great streamlined and silently operating turbines—the whole thing magically illuminated with a shadowless light from an oval window at the top. Here reigns a silence so absolute that it invites to panic. Where am I? Who am I? Is there no way out?

Yes, of course. In the background another automatic sliding door opens. It leads through three elegantly vaulted corridors into a kind of electric control room full of cabinets and complicated control panels, divided into regular sections with glass panes between them, so that you can see yourself constantly at various angles as if you were in a hall of mirrors. This has a refreshing and reassuring effect at first, like some grand joke—until you discover that it is a labyrinth and that you are lost in its endless spirals.

Then begins a terrified search for an exit, a senseless flight in which you constantly come face to face with your own desperate features and strike your forehead and knee against your hated image in the relentless glass—but in the distance there is a loud girlish laughter that echoes merrily through the endless curves of the labyrinth, draws nearer, grows warm and close, full of release. . . .

"Where did you go to?"

(Great, manifold echo as in a ravine.)

"Here!"

(Echo.)

"Run out through the emergency exit to the left! Hurry!"

(Echo.)

Yes, quite right—there is actually an emergency door here (EXIT, in pale violet neon letters). I open the door to a completely dark abyss—the ocean or outer space or whatever it may be. I sail out into the darkness in a wide curve, slowly descending as if on wings. It gives me a curious feeling of relief, a glorious tingling courses through my entire nervous system, I am swallowed up by great, silent masses of moisture, feel myself sublimely enveloped in the hidden crops of a million-year-old ocean bottom—a thicket of fleshy flowers, vibrant tentacles and muscular fans, half tissue and half spirit—all this intense and enchanted flora that covers the dark depths of creation.

Here is my home, here I am submerged and mercifully obliterated—quite confident that I shall be resurrected.

Still another nightmare (or whatever I should call it, for as things now stand I actually have difficulty in telling dreams from reality)—still another *spectacle imaginaire* must finally be recorded.

Finally? Sounds ominous. Am I really that far gone?

Oh, well—never mind. We'll let the curtain rise.

The Doomsday Machine has arrived. It was much smaller than I had imagined it, no larger than an ordinary transistor, very simple in appearance, a metal case with a handle, much like a handbag, with two plastic-covered indentations in the cover—one containing a sort of spray nozzle, the other a push-button. According to the instructions it was just a matter of removing the plastic protection and pressing the button. Very simple. So why hesitate, now that you've just about reached the goal of your most ardent wishes?

Well, is there actually such a terrible hurry? I asked myself, pouring myself a glass of Apage.

I had a feeling that there was still something lacking. Certain formalities. The blowing of trumpets—or what? What does one do when one cuts the silken thread and lets the Sword of Damocles fall? What did they do in Germany before they opened the valves of the gas chambers? What did the American president do before he sent his load of atom bombs to the unhappy cities of the yellow islanders?

"A moment of prayer!" suggests my *alter ego*, his voice strangely mild.

I glanced at him, almost had trouble recognizing him in his new, light Pharisee costume with a coquettish rose in the buttonhole. Smooth-shaven. Smoking a cigarette. Straw hat and walking stick. Hair slicked down. Whom did he remind me of? Buchman? Truman?

He took my arm, mildly remonstratively, patronizingly—the way a chief ego looks after a subordinate functionary-type ego. Had we switched roles?

"Get away from here!" I roared.

"Now, now—easy does it!" he said in a friendly way, quite unaffected. "Shall we *pray*?"

I gave him a helplessly hate-filled look. The worst had really happened; he had swung himself up to the position of a superego and apparently had full control of the field. Here I stood—deposed, reduced to the position of his hireling and helper. Here I stood with my ape-like wildman's face. Here stood the bitten-up, leprose ape with its swollen, throbbing wrist, its poisoned blood, and its mortally tortured soul.

But my fine superior lay kneeling in front of the Doomsday Machine with folded hands. He had placed a newspaper under his knees to protect his well-pressed, light trousers. He had placed his cigarette at the edge of the table; it lay there sending a long, carefree spiral of smoke into the air.

He was *praying*. I heard him use the phrase "these my little ones."

Meanwhile, it turned out that we were not alone. There was a third person present: my friend the stained-glass master Benedict. He was in a sorry state, still only half real, had practically only hands and heart, and a tired smile in an otherwise featureless face—a withered smile of the kind you see in ancient weathered statues or on the unfortunate victims of napalm. He told me with an almost inaudible voice, which went to my marrow, what an evil fate had befallen him. Everything had gone wrong. A bomber on patrol had made a terrible mistake and laid the cathedral in ruins; the faithful dog Prosper had been hit in the head by a falling crucifix and in an attack of madness had torn little Rosvita to pieces; her mother had joined the *flagellantes* in her anguish and was prostrate with exultant laughter after being raped by one of the sectarians.

I poured a glass of *vin cuit* for this unhappy rudiment of a human being, and this he eagerly drained, whereupon he disappeared with a puff.

My tyrant had risen from his position of prayer. He gave me an infinitely pleasant and understanding, but absolutely commanding look.

Now then—in God's name!

I squirmed and gnashed my teeth, but had to obey. Flung open the doors to the seething hell of the unoccupied parlors (a cross between the traffic roar of a modern city and a satanical allegory by Hieronymus Bosch), took the instrument of destruction in, removed the plastic covers, and pushed the button.

Nothing happened.

The whole thing was just a fake then, I thought as I woke up. . . .

Broad daylight. I was lying on the divan—alone. On the dirty table a battery of empty bottles and a couple of overturned glasses.

Evening.

The real insecticide machine arrived this afternoon, but now I won't have the means to pay for its delivery. Well, who cares. It will have to be sent back.

The shopkeeper, or rather his wife, for it was Madame Frelon I talked to, wouldn't even consider lending me any money. Not a *sou*. She laughed at me: I had been warned, had to take the consequences now of my stupid carelessness. She wouldn't even give me a bottle of *vin cuit* on credit. I had apparently enjoyed more of that product than was good for me, she insinuated. Wouldn't lend me the telephone, either, so that I would be able to ring up a friend in Paris and ask him to send me money for a ticket.

Would she in that case at least lend me a postage stamp so I could send a letter?

No. Madame Frelon gave an excited laugh and pierced my miserable and overgrown person with a barb of her merciless look. But then Monsieur Frelon came and handed me a tattered old postcard with a stamp on it.

Here you are. Write. We are not mean—merely firm in our principles. You may certainly have a loaf of bread and a piece of sausage on credit too.

A bottle of *vin cuit?* Or just *vin du pays?*

He glanced at his wife (appealingly, it seemed to me). She shook her head. Adamantly. He shook his head too, without meeting my eye.

Midnight.

The air is cool tonight. A fresh western breeze is blowing in from the Atlantic. Splendid sky twinkling with stars.

Got my postcard off. Went for a short evening walk in the heavenly landscape. The sickle of the new moon above the snow-covered mountain ridges to the south, flanked by Arcturus and Jupiter—a beautiful triad!

When I got back there were two bottles of country wine standing on my table, and in addition bread and cheese and a large *saucisse.* So Monsieur Frelon's good heart has won, then.

Have tidied the room and eaten my supper. Am sitting here now smoking my pipe and taking stock of my situation.

Must admit the whole thing after all looks brighter.

The swelling on my wrist is nearly gone. Wonder if the effects of that *mitavenin* bite aren't beginning to wear off, too?

Anyway, I have the feeling that I'm returning to my normal self again. And my inspiration is beginning to come back. In fits and starts. I really must see about reorganizing my ruined play! Still have my good ballpoint pen and lots of paper—can do without that noisy old machine.

It's more peaceful here, too, now that Gloire is gone and the heat wave has moved on. Only a few flies—hardly any mosquitoes.

Maybe I should simply drop those silly ideas about leaving?

Anyway, I can sleep on it.

Good night.

SIX PROSE POEMS

JIMMY SANTIAGO BACA

IT GOES BY MANY NAMES

And behind the eyeball it sucks it empty, scrapes it dry of sight like a kitchen pan, scoured silver and hard. But not like before, when the heart would pick up its drumsticks and pound the eyes like drums, or scoop up water from rivers in healthy perceptions, not these eyes.

They dangle in skulls like little iron bells set for ritual, some bewitching ceremony:

Blood in glass tubes rising; teeth clenching and that rag knotted round the arm, bloating blood vessels, to a plump swell of purple, pierced by a shiny needle, and the heroin slides in, mixes with heart's life, across its cheek like a sudden unfelt gash, opening to emptiness, to a dizzy shower of darkness, smoothing across mind, a flooding lake with barest ripples ribbing themselves through muscles, ironing them out to sagging tired meat, in the warm heat of heroin.

This is the new King.

His whip so gentle on bones of my people. His voice luring, seductive in its slow torture. It is our flesh that covers him with warmth, and our legs that carry him over mountains.

His black seed in the womb of our blood, like a black sun whose sunrays are our very blood, and splintered lives, spreading out over everything, into the hurting eyes of our loved ones, its dark glow, glowing.

So few can rebel against his mothering chains, suckling grains from his breasts, and pain from his fingertips.

When he leaves, the land is cold, and when present, how very warm and beautiful. Each bough a black, blossom blacker, until nothing is seen, nothing, there is nothing, the last flicker fading, into the King's cup, who drinks up lives, and lives, and lives.

And all the drug centers, the counselors, the prison sentences, the ravages upon society, upon families, upon the future, all of these, are like dry leaves under its golden boot, like sweet meat to its burly hungers, like sails under its wind, blowing us all further into its dark sea.

All my people are behind bars for taking heroin. But they are not criminals. They are under its spell, as others are under the spell of money, ambition, lucrative living, as others want to learn secrets of wisdom, as those under the horrors of jealousy: *they* are not criminals; or are they?

Nixon points his finger, the atom bomb points, the tearing up of earth points, the dirtying of our waters points, and so I point, not to my people, they are not criminals, I point to our ignorance, our shambled souls, our greed and easy living, our dull minds.

Cry and scream to me, You Are Wrong! Wrong! Wrong! And I will listen to you, and look long upon your face, and weep for you, be silent for you, assist you. And together, none of us being wrong, I will take your hand, and we will find our solutions, and the Great King will be no more, or will hobble on crutches and beg for crumbs at each gate of our wise culture, and be turned away, to hide in the hills, where now we imprison our brothers and sisters.

I ASK MYSELF, SHOULD I CRY? OR LAUGH?

I am like a glossy green leaf, sticking out
in midnight moon, waxy drumskin the moon pounds with
wind . . .

Guilt itches my heart, as though a grass-
hopper, chewing half, or a thick lazy caterpillar spinning silk
nets, hanging blue raindrops, baskets that carry invisible
rocks, that crack their stomachs, making wings of my eyelids.

Should I cry or laugh, thinking of you,
you?

An old woman on bent legs and burning
green eyes, what did you do on Saturday afternoons, in your
small trailer? Like a whitening sandbar, as the days took
more and more of your dark healthy grains, pressing against
the current of age, your tongue printed in sand washed over
silently by water, malevolent water, a ripple washing your
thunder-jeweled life, under, under, sweet pearl of mine.

Mother of my mother, after being moved
away, a small child clutching pennies you gave me, from a
purse hidden and hooked with a pin, next to your
breasts. . . .

You showed me a picture of my mother,
said she was a good woman, and pictures of my uncles, killed
in wars, their airplanes hut-hut hut-hutting out, hurtling
down the blue gray sky in a screaming crying fire.

I saw their pictures, all of them, but
when you showed the one of my mother, a blast exploded in
me, a white flare of love, cascading down my naked soul, as
though a waterfall, in which I bathed.

But you? Your trailer in a weedy lot, cro-
cheting tablecloths rich as butterfly wings, pillowcases de-
signed as sun spreading on dawn-colored silk, thick-fingered
frontiering heart in your wild loneliness, bad-mouthing my
father's drunkenness softly,

in your little trailer, with a toaster, cloth
pot-handles, tiny-windowed low-ceilinged box, a jewel case
to you, where your memories sang from each night . . .
I wanted to stay with you forever! To find
the truth, to ask and ask and ask, an Orphan Boy! swirling
with stallion storms in me!
I could not ride, set free into your wood-
wind throat, that sang me calm in your great box canyon,
dripping water, and silence that shined in our eyes;
our love, our confusion, our fears, tumbled
like massive boulders down our red-veined hearts,
thousands and thousands of years old,
covering the shards and death-skulls of your life,
holding the ocean of my future, my prehistoric hunger
for gods and demons unleashed, satiated by you Weaver
Woman.
You died while I was in prison,
This poem is for you, my one.

IN MY LAND

Time gets lost. You see it like the spurt of
a match in the night, and then it is suddenly blotted out
black under the sun.
The old people remember yesterday, the
women when their skirts got wet crossing the streams, the
men wood smoke in their hair and sap of piñon trees on their
hands.
But you look up, and where grandfather's
guns used to hang, now books stand, their pages yellowed.
A dog howls outside
at red evening. The windmill creaks. The mud is fresh with
cow hooves. There is a broken-down bus, and among weeds,
rusty frames of 32's and wooden plow handles, and a grave
or two with paper flowers pink and withered, rain stained.

In this land there is a graveness, of color
and heart. Here the white sands cannot absorb the rich blood
that sun sponges light from,
here wounds open in the heart like cracks
in a mountainside, here there is a solitude in each person, like
a cave where a portion of the person sits and thinks.

Cattle move lazily to troughs. You cannot
put a price on a land where grass burns a green fire
that blinded my heart when young, and now gives it sight.
You cannot shout down the voice of water,
when over parched clay it whispers,
licking its wounded children of roots.

The cities here have grown large. When
you visit a girl, watch out for your muddy boots on the car-
pet. And if you smell like sheep and coyote you better wash,
for the city will not understand you.

There is a tv in every house. And when
you sit there, waiting to take out your girl, the wind from the
window will give you strength to change, or meet the change.

There is college, and parties, and neigh-
borhoods with old wood and whistling boys, and people will
cross cultural barriers, holding up their arms protecting what
little they own, some will drown from their innocence,
and blackest hair ever will flag wildly in
breeze, you will believe nothing so beautiful has ever been,
and as myself, you will be born again and
again, in this land, to carry the pain of change, the courage
of love, like the mountain over the valley, we must have the
courage
of love, to live.

I AM WHO I AM

You ask me what has happened to the woman I love,
If I still love her. . . . I smile a lot to that question,
A good and soft smile. I wonder myself about that question,
And that is why I smile. What has happened to her?
She is slowly grafting herself into a woman.
I have fond memories of her. For the rest, all I know,
is that I will live alone in this life,
though I constantly try to convince myself otherwise.
Loneliness follows me through crowds like my own shadow
crossing over faces and bodies of the multitudes in the sun.
Into the distance in myself I walk away, over the sanddunes
and through the mirages I walk into the distance and die.
There are many worlds in me; though virile and young,
I cannot conquer them. Gripped by the teeth,
by the words of a shaman, at the same time a romantic poet,
at the same time a priest and lover of the body,
at the same time a farmer, I speak through all of them,
a village developed by them all in one-ness I am,
so my home is their home, my food is their food.

But I was offered this or that, life or death,
and a third alternative: in a vision I was offered understanding
of the spiritual world. I, however, in my ignorance, and
love of life, chose to experience the movement of a little finger,
experience what people experience, from the tiny movement
of their lips, to their sighing death breath, with all my
human frailty and futility, in my ignorance, I chose
that it will be by my hand that my life is carved and fragmented.

Love me in a way that is suited to you. If you must build walls
then build them. You are free to do as you wish.
All people in life are. I will not supplicate others not to do
what they are doing. Each wall is different
and each person is different, but they are never so high
that the sunshine will not enter inside. Try like hell,
and still the sunshine will enter them.

Human beings are fantastic pavilions, tents you see in the night;
the glow of youth, beauty or money illuminates their faces,
but still inside, we see a shadow pass behind the canvas eye,
still inside is where the test begins, to understand one's self,
a very old man and very young child, constant and changing,
despising the same things that are loved,
in its fervid beautiful crazy confusion,
dazed in its romance of the world, tragic in its ridiculous sadness,
giving miracles to friends because it cannot give itself away,
living with loneliness that gives it all it needs,
setting a plate of vegetables before the child,
asking the old man to wrestle mountains,
in this way finding out who we are.

THROUGH THE STREETS

Friday night whistles at young ladies, and
holds others close to its fat heart, where Barry White sings
on a wooden stool, in the cool smoke of feelings.

The Friday fields free themselves of
week-long work, and white flowers fly from their hands, and
lovers lie across the dips and grooves of grass.

Through the town, Friday rides. With
lights on and music extra fired from horns and strings, the
streets sink to a welcome passage, and fit the crowds and
gaudy glare of grime and gold.

People plunge into the wave of late-night
fun, and run their hearts on oily streaks, and dance on a dime
or spin to the tune of a blues, and chuck the rhymes of
weekly ringing bells and raging presidents, duck the world
like a bishop in his mirroring clothing, and in robes and per-
fumes and pleasant hails, huddle with crowds to crown the
night with light.

The blinding light of town does not
bother you, for it's the night that Jumbo Balloons sail over
stadiums, and worked-on cars tear their tires on streets to the
sweet giggle of growing bosoms.

Yes, the Wizard waves his wand, and unafraid, the soft appearance of people forms around us. It is the night, when homes are sold for a drink, a woman for a shot of heroin and a pack of smokes, a thousand and thousand more, sexy the night, and the young lover carries a thousand hearts, and the old a thousand and thousand more.

Each State, each town, each small home, drinks up, decks out, and cards themselves to the stars, that sit around in glowing robes, and explode in frustrated fire, and curse across the night sky, unable to answer why, in droves, we undream the hours, and take our blood in hand, and let it sing, and cry, and laugh and scream.

For tomorrow we dream, and the stars will be sane again.

But tonight, tonight is Friday. It is to the people, like fish to the hungry horded before the lord's feet. It is the miracle that walks the bloody week in pure love, it is the rest one gets from its breath, invigorating our weak frames to the stature of Gods, followers of Gods, whose kingdom is within them, vulnerable, shatterable, conquerable.

In the sky the moon is a dragon guarding the galaxy. And we below in dark bars, ooze to the blues, make magic of men, wine of women, and throw our hair into night's hand, that dyes it gray or young young black, in the morning when we wake.

Saturday, we feel like warriors, women and men, gently walking the grounds in light clothing. Our horses feed in the fields. And already we are thinking of the war come Monday.

IT'S GOING TO BE A COLD WINTER

A batch of new guards, trained to sniff out brittle tip-ends of straw brooms, packed into my cell this morning.

Door barely open; like a sleepy slave on the run, sweating on a cotton mattress, my eyes open frightened, then aware, and focusing on solid faces, summer-burned red, I crawl out of bed.

I stand up: one pats my legs, the pads of my hard feet, runs his hands beneath my balls, over my penis, up along my ribs, under my armpits, in my ears fingers dig, through my hair they crawl, and then, like cargo tied and wound up with suspicious eyes, I am placed aside.

They enter my cell: a legal pillow fight begins with my books and papers. Stir-crazy madmen, papers sidling down to cement floor, my mattress turned over, sheets torn away like a mask hiding tons of heroin; but nothing, only cotton, cheap sweaty moldy smelling cotton, picked by slaves, sewed up by slaves, slaves of the Greater State, that come in all colors.

My books are leafed through, I imagine, hounddogs howling up a tree at some paragraph of wild bird or squirrel. They ravish up my poems in folders, their eyes scan the blood and misery I write about that is here, the disrespect for our human bodies and emotions, they lick with long steady tongues, on the other side of my experience, a badge between us, like a door as tall and guarded as any of heaven's for rebuking sinners.

I can see their teeth and their eyes. Something greater holds them in tow, and human words cannot pull them away. Something drives them to do what they are doing. It's not gold anymore, as it was with their fathers, it's them, so small, they fit themselves among fraternities of terror, growing suddenly, losing their place as humans, to become polished boots and black club dangling from belts.

They laugh like homeboys loving mom's apple pie. Good American men. Behind their shades (they all wear sunglasses), their eyes turn gray, and I imagine some ghostly farmer as their souls, holding up an ancient rifle, saying, "Atta boy, attta boy. Get em boy, dadgumit, get em!" And the guards, ever quickly scrambling through my belongings.

Bankers sit themselves before dark-red rich oak desks. New fresh dresses are put on by women. Breakfast scents drape the morning air. School children giggle, pass through shortcuts to school, while the earth almost seems to soften their passage, sprinkling dew about, dogs to run, trees to swoosh their leaves, young lovers to smile with the moon's mellow lips. Healthy workers enjoying coffee, talking trade stuff, and utility bills. Streets adorned with shops, and people gesturing with hands, and doors shutting, and the bulky growl of cars sputtering up for a spin around the block to pick up some lard, flour, sugar, and eggs, at the corner grocery.

And I'm standing here in my boxer shorts, my hair like Bozo the clown, my soul a gigantic tent, filled with the circus of life, the elephants sounding, and the escaped tigers bursting from my cage, to tell me, "OK. We're done."

BURIED ALIVE

RAMÓN HERNÁNDEZ

Translated from the Spanish by María Castellanos Collins and Margaret E. Beeson

The choir of apterous angels, not winged, indeed nocturnal, pale, was assembled around the winged angel indeed I want, indeed I always desire in the midst of night that sweet water that says truth, I am free, I love an instant which does not weaken beside the sea or the eye of the unknown friend, possessor of a soul, never of just a framework. It was, I say, assembled around me. On their shoulders, like something formerly noble, rested tunics and chlamys, shameful silences and bribes, clannish labyrinths: this man yes, this man no, that one is conveniently mute, or deaf, or blind, or paralyzed.

The choir was, I repeat in silence, comfortably installed in its seats of the semicircular pyramid. Their expressions revealed fear, haughtiness, that breath of those who are perishable. Never a sea yes I die never you die. As they were thus arranged, I heard with great clarity the sound of a bell. The president, a weak and blue looking old man, made an ambiguous gesture excuse me, I wish would be to get up, but it is impossible. And he said:

"The session is now open."

A dying sun shone on the hand of the attorney or prosecutor I adorn myself with my wig, I clear my throat, I cough, I take a lozenge, another one, a second coughing spell, a certain "by your leave."

"You may begin."

"Thank you, Mister President."

As he looks, I nod my head, I say: amen. And addressing me: "The defendent will rise."

A momentary weakness kept me a second on the hard bench where the winged angels are chained, in front of the inexorable judges. The prosecutor became impatient they call me "your grace." I am honorable, I ride in the wingless victory chariot.

"Obey," he ordered in his inharmonious, useless voice that was extinguished in the echo of the room.

"Your pardon," I murmured.

But, immediately, I regretted having asked pardon for my torpor and corrected energetically:

"In reality, I do not beg your pardon. I simply say, I am sorry."

The wingless court reporter I do not think, I only take down words, never the poem that moves the spirit, also corrected without complaining it is indifferent to me, I am earning a living. I hate them all.

"You are a bit impertinent," commented the prosecutor.

And, casting me a glance dark as pitch, he added:

"You are absurd."

Arching his brows, he adjusted his glasses I wear glasses from studying so much I have myopia, I am myopic, and he consulted my file with bitterness: it is impossible to be benign, these angels with wings are the ruin of the country and of civilization. Finally, he said:

"You are accused of indeed I want, indeed I always desire in the midst of night that water that says truth, I am free, I love an instant which does not weaken beside the sea or the eye of the unknown friend possessor of a soul, never of just a framework. Right?"

"Yes, sir," I responded.

"Say: yes, your grace," he admonished me.

"Yes, your grace," I said.

The choir of apterous angels, not winged indeed nocturnal, pale, was assembled in the same attitude of mummies wearemummies.

Continue gentleman, proceed your grace, do not let the prosecutor interrupt the trail of this defendant who claims to be a winged angel, a friend of Liberty and Love. Finish him off rapidly and let us move on to golf, bridge, morphine, the dollar, the hand that strangles and the voice listen, innocent ones, what I say to you is a convenient lie let's finish him off.

"In such a case," continued the prosecutor I always accuse. "Explain to the choir what you understand by indeed I want, indeed I always desire in the midst of night that water that says etc., etc., etc., . . . What does framework mean?"

I realized that my life was in danger and was ready to defend myself with my whole being. I wanted to live under the skin and the wind, with my eyes fixed on the impregnable sky and my thoughts concentrated on the expression brothers, we are happy the Eternal is not a dream of the mind, we have wings. The choir, nevertheless, moved closer together, a hostile group we are insatiable, this winged angel who brings words instead of dollars, lies or pettiness pains us grievously. No. No. We do not have wings, there is no Eternal One, it is a dream of the mind. Any agitator who deceives the people saying "you have wings" will be eliminated.

I began, "Brothers, I only want to tell you that there is a thirst of liberty and a longing for love in that poor hand which at break of day, grasps the hose of the sanitation department and whispers let's go water the street, the avenue, let's go sweep the huge city, let's clean it for the others, for the trail from the mines, and for the vertigo of the scaffolds where men freeze as do the bitter voice of the cancer and the kiss of the public woman I have nothing, I have no identity card, I have not. There is a thirst of liberty and a longing for love in this quiet life of our people, there are wings for these angels, there are flights of eternity in each death . . ."

While I was speaking, I observed the faces of the choir of apterous angels, not winged, indeed nocturnal, pale. Lethal anger chokes us, winged exterminating angel.

"Go on."

"I only want to tell you that the hour has arrived to go out naked onto the deserted beach, to populate it with our voices, with our eyes, with our wings, oh child come oh child, the demoniacal antibaby will not be a mother, the home will not be a martyrdom you will not be a metalic electronic you, nor the hypnotic brother of opium, nor the decomposition of the intoxication of the automobile-mass, things, materials which are bought and sold. The businessman will not be a wolf, nor the factory lathes of horror, strident sounds, my love, my head aches, my soul a rotating lathe aches, I am not free, your are not free when you love, you are not free when you cry, I am not free you are not free when you dream the chain from sunup to sundown a constant shadow of the earth binds you, you will never finish that block of miserable dwellings there on the outskirts of the city, you will never stop moving propelled by the hand of the angels without wings, without that thirst for love that filled the minds of heroes, you are not a free slave, you are not a free voice which may break the boundary of prejudices that tortures this country where in days gone by winged angels were numerous, multitudes that open mouths are hungry are cold make war die have childish legs like corn stalks, you are not free, your grace, you are not free neither the judges nor the defendants are free, because not having wings you are not true angels and things, like water, will seep through your fingers and the last day will be a hymn of horror I am afraid, where is the bungalow, the Oldsmobile, the glittering lady, the perfume of the lady and the real estate I speculate? Apartments, commissions, people in lines, people in silence, people in dreams will drag you into the sewers—oh angels without wings!—apterous, not winged, indeed nocturnal, pale from the dollar and the lie always the lie, I warn you: Death will arrive and that thirst for peace and love it will no longer be possible to drink the water that says truth, I am free, I love the instants which do not weaken beside the sea or the eye of the unknown friend possessor of a soul never of just a framework. Nevertheless, I swear to you all: there is an Eternal One, there are angels with wings who . . .

A viscous wave of protest court reporter, I order you, do not transcribe that, let it not be placed in the records, that heretic is raving, he is a fool, rose like a column of smoke to the dome. The choir of apterous angels, not winged, indeed nocturnal, pale, descended the steps like an inundation with their arms raised. Some, the most excited ones, tore their chlamys, the bowels of the earth we are earth without wings we are dollars.

"Do away with him!," they shouted.

"Let us eliminate him!"

Meanwhile when they were finally restrained by the guards, the atonic voice of the president could scarcely be heard:

"Let the defendant proceed, but be brief, please."

That was all very dreary to him I know it all. Always, since the far away times of my youth and childhood, I have also been a child, there has surged forth the voice of some prophet blessed ones, have faith, look at the stars, search in your hearts for the wings of Love and Liberty. And the same thing has occurred:

"Let the defendant continue."

The angry faces, that implacable choir which hated me, filled my soul with sadness and I said I am dying. I prefer dying to debasing myself by supplicating. The prosecutor puckered his lips I despise you, winged angel I hate you, I hate myself, I need to forget that time when I too was like you, you will be eliminated from this country of angels without wings and I will sleep in peace, we will sleep, choir, we will sleep, have patience and let him finish.

"Let him," repeated his grace, "let him, I promise you that his crime will not go unpunished."

The breath of the choir heated the mercury of its hatred we are horrified by the winged angel we remain in the pyramidal hemicycle in appearance but, in the depth of our beings, there are tears, shame dollar shame, oh child, oh demoniacal antibaby mother, oh shrapnel in the bodies of the combatants napalm, jungle, we don't know why we are fighting, why the hate.

"In reality, I have little to say to you," I continued despondently, "I tried to make you understand that there are wings, that there is love and liberty, that an Eternal One exists never the sanguinary beast the gold, the deceit. That tragic and anguished shadow of living is a shadow and there is an eternity waiting in each death . . ."

I was not able to finish. The choir of apterous angels, not winged, indeed nocturnal, pale, fused into an implacable mob that grabbed me from the bench where the angels with wings are chained and, not heeding the voice of the president and the voice of the prosecutor and the voice of conscience is a terrible voice, which counseled patience, gentlemen, patience, we have a code of laws, a professional executioner who will carry out the sentence, death, the final punishment, ignoring those voices, they buried me alive.

TWO CONCRETE POEMS

DICK HIGGINS

snowflake: dark room, dark rose

dark
is
it
dark room
dark rose
what color?
dark rose
a
dark room
in a
sleeping
is
it
what color?
it
is
sleeping
in a
dark room
a
dark rose
what color?
dark rose
dark room
it
is
dark

nyc
20.iv.78

the ſnowflakes of giordano bruno

"chooſing MIND to see"

i

the   things
the little things
woo'd
woo'd by form
form
by
form
the little things woo'd
form
by
little   form
by
great
chooſing
great
by
little   form
by
form
the little things woo'd
form
by
form
woo'd by form
woo'd
the little things
the   things

ii

and
IS
the river
the billion drops of water?
and all
the movement between the ſhores?
and all and all
the place where terrence drowned?
and all and all and all
the billion
and
the place
and
the movement
the river
THE MIND'S EYE
'S
THE EYE
'S
MIND
'S
THE EYE
'S
THE MIND'S EYE
the river
the movement
and
the place
and
the billion
and all and all and all
the place where terrence drowned?
and all and all
the movement between the ſhores?
and all
the billion drops of water
the river
IS
and

iii

to ſee
to ſee the largeneſs
and to be like the largeneſs
to be like the ſmallneſs
like
the largeneſs
like
the ſmallneſs
like
to like the largeneſs
the ſmallneſs
to ſee
each ſpinning world
in its own
and infinite
infinite ſpinning
acting in harmony with the vaſt
to ſee
acting in harmony with the vaſt
infinite ſpinning
and infinite
in its own
each ſpinning world
to ſee
the ſmallneſs
to like the largeneſs
like
the ſmallneſs
like
the largeneſs
like
to be like the ſmallneſs
and to be like the largeneſs
to ſee the largeneſs
to ſee

october 23rd, 1977
new york

NOTES ON CONTRIBUTORS

BETSY ADAMS, who is working toward her Ph.D. in evolutionary ecology, has had two books of poetry published to date. Her long-range goals, she says, include the implementation of alternatives to the uses of living animals in biomedical research and related areas and, of course, the continuation of her writing.

"real estate" is one of a series of related "talk pieces" from a forthcoming book, *Tuning*, that, says DAVID ANTIN, "explores the relations between discovery and knowing and coming to a common knowledge." These pieces push the talk pieces further along the lines of story narrative and intelligent discourse proposed in *Talking at the Boundaries* (New Directions, 1976).

JIMMY SANTIAGO BACA, now in his mid-twenties, was born in New Mexico and has also lived south of the border. He has recently been in the state prison in Florence, Arizona, but was paroled a few months before the appearance of this volume. A book of his poems is to be published by Louisiana State University Press. Baca's work was brought to their—and ND's—attention by Denise Levertov, who takes some pride in her "discovery."

PETER BALAKIAN lives in Providence, Rhode Island, where he teaches at Brown University. He also edits, with Bruce Smith, *Graham House Review*, a biannual magazine devoted to contemporary poetry. His "Seven Poems" are part of a collection in progress titled *Father Fisheye*.

LAWRENCE FERLINGHETTI's City Lights Books, long a mecca for the West Coast avant-garde and a spearhead of the San Francisco renaissance of the 1950s, recently celebrated its twenty-fifth anniversary. His *Northwest Ecolog* (City Lights) appeared last year, and he is now preparing a new, major collection for New Directions.

Information on WILLIAM HEINESEN will be found in the translator's note preceding his story "The Flies." HEDIN BRØNNER, who has taught at several American universities and published numerous studies on Scandinavian literature, now divides his time between the United States and his native Norway. He is the author of *Three Faroese Novelists* (1972), the compiler-translator of *Faroese Short Stories* (1973), and the translator of Heinesen's *The Kingdom of the Earth* (1974), all brought out by Twayne.

Born in Madrid in 1935, RAMÓN HERNÁNDEZ works as an engineer at the Institute for the Conservation of Nature. He is, by vocation, a painter, though he has written one drama, published seven novels, and contributed his short fiction to Spanish literary journals. MARÍA CASTELLANOS COLLINS and MARGARET E. BEESON teach in the Department of Languages at Kansas State University.

DICK HIGGINS, a poet and critic, spends most of his time in Vermont. Among his many published books are *For Eugene in Germany* (Unpublished Editions, 1974) and *A Book About Love & War & Death* (Something Else Press, 1972).

Born in Paterson, New Jersey, in 1953, PETER KURINSKY attended the State University of New York at Purchase and Brown University, where he was a student of John Hawkes. "The Investigation" is his first published story.

JAMES PURDY's short play *True* (*ND34*) was produced at the 1978 Summer Festival of New York's Westbeth Theatre Center, while in November of the same year the Ensemble Studio Theatre performed dramatized versions of stories from his two early collections, *Color of Darkness* and *Children Is All*, as well as a new play, *Clearing in the Forest*. The New London Press (Dallas, Texas) is publishing a paperback collection of seven of his plays this year, plus the short story "How I Became a Shadow" (*ND36*).

An appreciation of ALEKSEI REMIZOV (1877–1957) precedes his "Eight Drawings." ALEKSIS RANNIT, who introduces these graphics by the influential Russian novelist and short story writer, is an Estonian poet who has lived in the United States since 1953. Translations of his verse have appeared in *ND24, ND25,* and *ND32* and been collected in three separate volumes: *Cantus Firmus* (1978) and *Donum Estonicum* (1976), both from the Elizabeth Press, and *Line* (1970), published by Adolf Hürlimann (Zurich).

JULIA OLDER has translated all of the stories and a score of poems by the late BORIS VIAN (1920–59). Her own work has been published in various literary journals. She is the author, with Steve Sherman, of *Appalachian Odyssey* (Stephen Greene Press, 1977), about her hike along the length of the two-thousand-mile Appalachian Trail.

A frequent contributor to these pages, PAUL WEST received the *Paris Review*'s Aga Khan Prize for fiction in 1974. His most recent novels include *Colonel Mint* (Dutton, 1972) and *Gala* (Harper & Row, 1976), and his latest, *Stauffenberg,* is due from Harper & Row some time this year.